GARDENING
WITH
COLOUR

GARDENING
WITH
COLOUR

LANCE HATTATT

p

This is a Parragon Book
This edition published in 2001

Parragon
Queen Street House
4 Queen Street
Bath BA1 1HE, UK

Conceived, edited, illustrated
and produced by Robert Ditchfield Publishers

Text and illustrations copyright © Parragon 2001
Photographs copyright © Robert Ditchfield 2001
This edition copyright © Parragon 2001

ISBN 0 75255 070 5

A copy of the British Library Cataloguing in Publication
Data is available from the Library.

Typeset by Action Typesetting Ltd, Gloucester
Colour origination by Colour Quest Graphic Services Ltd,
London E9
Printed and bound in China

Half Title: A bright late summer display of *Rudbeckia*.

Frontispiece: *Helenium* 'Moerheim Beauty' in dazzling
combination with *Allium spaerocephalon*.

Title Page: *Clematis viticella* 'Purpurea Plena Elegans'

Opposite: A subtle early summer combination of *Allium
christophii* against a background of purple cotinus and blue
Campanula latiloba.

THE AIM of this book is to provide the gardener with a tool to help him or her plan colour schemes in the garden.

Colour effects We respond differently to each colour and to combinations of colour. This book explains the effect of individual colours within a scheme.

Colour succession This book provides a wide range of plants through the seasons, with special sections on autumn and winter subjects.

SYMBOLS

Where measurements are given, the first is the plant's height followed by its spread. The following symbols are also used in this book:

○ = thrives best or only in full sun
◑ = thrives best or only in part-shade
● = succeeds in full shade
E = evergreen

Where no sun symbol and no reference to sun or shade is made in the text, it can be assumed that the plant tolerates sun or light shade.

Many plants are poisonous and it must be assumed that no part of a plant should be eaten unless it is known that it is edible.

Contents

Introduction	8
The Colour Wheel	16
Why Colour Varies	20
Using Colour in the Garden	24
Colours of the Spectrum	28
Yellow and Cream	30
Orange	46
Red	52
Pinks and Pastels	68
Purple and Lilac	88
Blue	104
Green	116
Variegation	126
White, Grey and Black	132
White	134
Grey	150
Black	158
Colour Combinations	160
Yellow with White	162
Yellow with Red	166
Yellow with Blue/Purple	168
Blue with White	172
Lavender with Pinks and Reds	176
Massed Colour	180
Colour in the Border	184
Autumn Colours	188
Autumn Foliage	190
Autumn Fruit and Berries	202
Bark and Stems	212
Colour Around the Garden	216
The Alpine and Rock Garden	218
The Kitchen Garden	222
The Water Garden	226
The Winter Garden	230
The Conservatory	234
Pots and Containers	238
Acknowledgements	246
Index	247

Right: A pastel combination for early summer – pale purple dictamnus set against *Rosa* 'Iceberg'.

GARDENING WITH COLOUR

The arrangement of colour in the garden has to be one of the most satisfying and pleasurable of all the aspects of gardening. It is in this area, more than most, that the gardener is able to find real expression, working with plants to create a living picture which will not only be aesthetically pleasing to others but which will be a fulfilment of a very personal, and often frustrating, striving. For unlike the painter who controls the colours of the palette, the gardener must for ever be subject to the variables of the weather, the caprice of the seasons and the complexity of the plants themselves. But it is in these very challenges that the thrill and excitement of working with colour are to be found.

WHY COLOUR MATTERS

So much time outdoors seems to be taken up with the seasonal tasks of endless weeding, pruning, deadheading, cutting grass, trimming edges, potting on, and similar mundane chores, that the placing of plants with regard to the maximum effect takes on a secondary role. If this is allowed to happen at all times, then one of the principal joys of the garden will be lost. Each one of us in visiting a garden, or in looking critically at our own, is aware first and foremost of the ways in which colour is used to heighten, complement or add to the design.

Gardeners, like artists, have always had a deep interest in colour and its effect in a garden setting. Gardeners like Gertrude Jekyll who made public her own innovative ideas on the use of colour in books like 'Colour in the Flower Garden' as well as articles such as 'Colour Effects in the Late Summer Border', have done much to influence the way in which we now think about these matters. Similarly the concept of the colour enclosure, the most famous of which is the white garden at Sissinghurst Castle created by Vita Sackville-West in the immediate post-war years, is something which has become firmly rooted in gardening tradition. Looking ahead to the future we see the highly original and bold use of

Broad sweeps of colour are used in this border.

Drifts of blue forget-me-nots and yellow poppies in a colour themed border.

White dominates this springtime planting.

colour arranged in massive drifts of a single plant currently being undertaken in a number of European countries as well as in America.

COLOUR EFFECTS

Planning colour in any garden is something which is totally individual, a matter of personal taste. Sometimes it is the work of a single person, more often than not it is a shared occupation. Always it is a case of one preference over another.

White gardens, or white borders, have, rather sadly, been over-done, resulting in a plethora of pale imitations of those which are generally regarded as being among the best. Now perhaps is the time to move on, to experiment with more original combinations where white, whilst

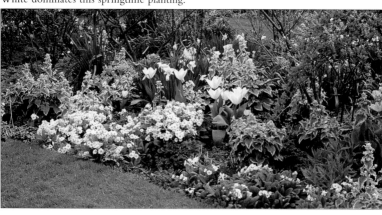

remaining the dominant colour, is used to contrast or to highlight other shades. For example, those who seek the reassurance of a cool, restful scheme may like to try marrying white with grey and silver. To this could be added, if desired, some of the cool blues. White with lemon, or a stronger gold, works well as does white against green. Whatever, there is room for movement away from the tried and tested schemes of the past towards something new, exciting and different.

Green is very much the colour of formality. Tightly clipped yew hedges, neatly arranged box-lined paths, topiary shapes together with carefully formulated foliage effects are all to be found in formal situations. Exceedingly small gardens, such as

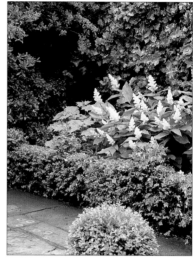

Here box provides formality.

Brick paths are marked with shaped domes.

Late summer and this border remains full of colour.

those to be had in larger towns and cities, lend themselves particularly well to this kind of treatment. Generally speaking, the smaller the area the more restricted should be the use of colour if a co-ordinated, harmonious effect is to be achieved.

Where a garden lends itself to division into outdoor rooms or enclosures, and these do not have to be of any great size, then much enjoyment may be had from creating a themed area which deliberately sets out to convey a particular atmosphere or mood. Colours for something along these lines will be very much a matter of individual taste, although some consideration should be given to what lies within the immediate surroundings. It would, of course, be a mistake to devise some scheme which upon completion would sit uneasily in its environment. Purples, mauves and blacks may be employed very successfully for a sombre, even melancholy effect, if that is what appeals. Certainly there are to be found some thought-provoking, Gothic gardens which make extensive use of these colours. On a brighter note, late summer herbaceous perennials may be gathered together into a hot garden, of strong reds and yellows, which will themselves suggest climates far removed from our own.

It would be totally wrong to indicate that success, or pleasing results, may only be had where shades of a single colour, or colours which work in harmony together, are used. There are many for whom massed floral displays, such as are to be found in public parks or, indeed, to decorate road schemes in urban areas, are a constant source of delight for their very brightness and cheerfulness. There is nothing at all wrong with using colour in this manner, although it has to be said that when applied to a domestic situation, then unless great care is taken the results can appear restless and confusing.

GARDENING WITH COLOUR

Very often it may prove necessary to alter the garden physically in order to execute a planned colour scheme. This may be as little as changing the shape of a border or constructing or planting a new division to form a background. On the other hand it may be far more radical like disposing of some existing feature to bring about a complete change to accommodate some new found interest.

Roses and clematis work together.

Some plants, and thus some colour effects, demand certain treatment. For those who carry a love for alpines, then it is first hand knowledge that these little jewels would be lost if left to their own devices in the main borders. To be really effective, and to give of their best, they need to be placed in such a way as to resemble as closely as possible their natural habitat. Devising such a situation, and then arranging them in pleasing colour groups to extend over as long a season as possible, is but just one of the ways in which colour is used in a practical manner. Roses, possibly more than any other shrubs, lend themselves to being grouped together. The continued popularity of the rose garden is evidence of this. Sadly, all too often, these gardens turn out to be little more than a nightmare of clashing colours where little, if any, thought has been given to the overall effect. This is such a pity for roses are ideal candidates to be partnered with all manner of wonderful complementary plantings.

Not many of us are fortunate enough to possess a wood. In early spring, when the canopy of leaves is down, early flowering treasures, such as the winter aconites, wild daffodils and primroses, could all be employed to provide a succession of colour based on a particular theme. Later the scheme could be varied, not only to maintain interest but to allow for later flowering shrubs and perennials.

A sunny site, which may not in itself be very large, could provide a splendid position in which to establish a tapestry carpet of thyme. These low-growing, perennial herbs, flowering over a long period, may be planted out, rather in the manner of a needlework picture, to satisfy with a rich array of colour. Depending on the plants chosen, the effect may be one of bright modernity or of faded antique. Full sun, and some shelter,

A skilfully arranged display.

may be the right conditions for growing many of the highly desirable, slightly tender perennials which are so much admired.

SEASONAL COLOUR

Each one of the four seasons, around which all gardening revolves, dictates to a certain extent its own colours. Springtime suggests in the main yellow, from the palest of lemons to the deepest of buttery shades. Most likely this is on account of the primroses of the hedgerow and the wealth of cheery daffodils which contribute so much pleasure in town and country gardens alike. But it is also the colour of catkins, of witch hazels

Flaming reds, oranges and yellows glow in a woodland area.

and, of course, of the flowers of the forsythia, a shrub which remains as popular as ever. As spring moves into summer, so pastel shades come into their own. Lilacs and roses, irises, campanulas, pale forms of oriental poppy, hardy cranesbill, alliums, lupins and delphiniums, the list is almost endless. Later it is the hot colours which seem to dominate, maybe in preparation for autumn which lies just around the corner.

As the year draws to a close so splendid autumnal foliage trails a blaze of fire throughout the countryside. Burnished leaves drifting through borders and piling into windswept corners possess their own particular charm. And whilst all of this, sadly, heralds the year's end, it is, not least because of the spectacular colour, both thrilling and exciting. Winter is not without considerable colour interest. Evergreens make a particularly valuable contribution for it is now, free of other border distractions, that they make their mark most clearly on the landscape. Deciduous trees and shrubs do not deserve to be overlooked. Bare branches and stems, etched against a winter sky, can look breathtakingly wonderful, particularly when dusted with hoar frost. Even the dying leaves of spent perennials add character to the garden in winter.

The Colour Wheel

Traditionally the colour wheel is made up of three primary colours, red, yellow and blue. By combining these together in equal quantity binary colours, or orange, green and violet, are produced. From mixing one or more of these all other colours are obtained. Colours on the wheel, as illustrated, divide into warm and cool areas. On the warm, or hot, side are red, orange and yellow, although it has to be admitted that lemon yellows cannot be considered hot. The remaining three colours, green, blue and violet, fall onto the cool side.

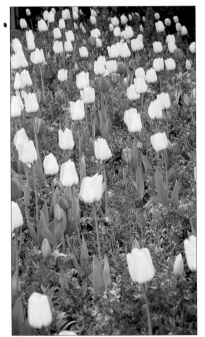

The hot side of the colour wheel.

Amongst the cool colours.

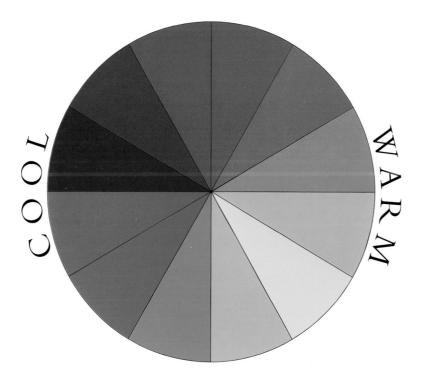

COOL

WARM

Those colours which are positioned next to each other and which have a pigment in common are said to be in harmony. For example, red and orange, yellow and green, blue and violet, these all harmonize together. Colours which appear opposite to each other on the colour wheel, often known as complementary colours, work together too. Red and green, yellow and violet, blue and orange will all complement each other although sometimes the contrast is not to everyone's taste. As a general rule, those colours which do not go together, or which do not appeal on an individual level, may be separated one from the other with the addition of white or grey.

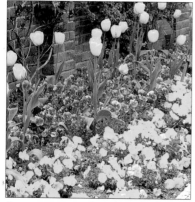

A strong contrast of pansies and tulips.

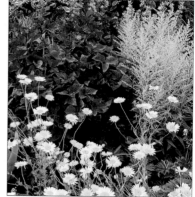

Deep purple as a foil to yellow.

Spires of yellow against soft pink.

Isoplexis sceptrum and *Verbascum* 'Helen Johnson'.

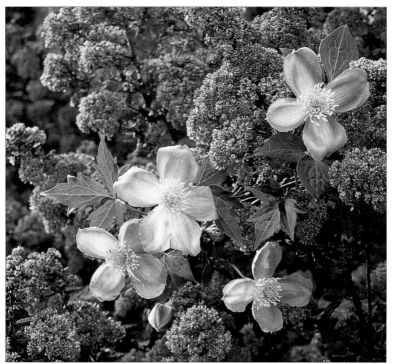

Pink and blue never fails to delight. Here *Clematis montana* 'Tetrarose' weaves its way through *Ceanothus* 'Puget Blue'.

The main disadvantage of the colour wheel is, of course, that it does not take into account all the varying tints in the garden. There are few violet flowers, and fewer red ones, when compared with the vast array of pink ones. Flower colour too may be considerably altered by the shape of the actual bloom as well as by texture, so that a mop-headed blossom is likely to deepen a shade whilst an ethereal, airy one will have the opposite effect. However, colour is all about individual taste and there are not, nor should there be, any hard and fast rules.

19

Why Colour Varies

Colour in nature is subject to so very many forces beyond the control of the individual that at times it would appear as if all success is a matter of chance.

Most difficult to combat is the effect of the weather. Brilliant hot sunshine can alter the appearance of colour in the garden just as much as intense cold or strong winds. Rain is by no means a neutral agent. The soft, refreshing showers of early spring serve, particularly when linked to warm sunlight, to heighten and intensify colours. This in direct contrast to autumnal days of solid rain when everything, seen under lowering, grey skies, becomes almost monochromatic.

Light levels alter as the seasons change. These in turn bring about alterations in the colour of leaves and

Kniphofia 'Sunningdale Yellow' brings a brilliance to a summer border.

Astilbes enhanced by their foliage.

White can be startling.

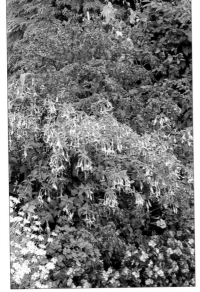

Fuchsias contribute colour in late summer.

A cool, restful scene.

flowers. Even within a single day it is possible to be aware of most noticeable differences in colour. The pH factor of the soil, that is to say the degree to which it is acid or alkaline, will also affect colour tone as will the colour instability to be found inherent in all plants.

The best possible means by which to counter all of these things is to be confident in plant knowledge. The experienced gardener will be sure of the habits, likes and dislikes of his or her plants. The beginner will be enthusiastic and quick to learn.

Winter colour with cyclamen and autumn crocuses.

Delphiniums make a statement of summer colour.

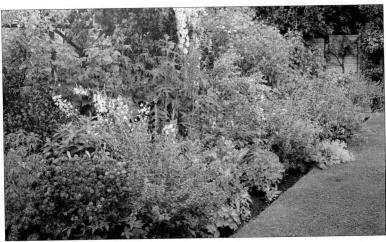

These soft colours of the early summer are in complete harmony.

A midsummer border where the colours are, in the main, muted.

Using Colour in the Garden

Few would deny that one of the principal concerns of gardening is the way in which colour is employed throughout the garden. What is perhaps less immediately obvious, and certainly open to debate, are the ways and means by which gardeners consciously utilize colour in order to achieve particular effects. These may in themselves be intentionally restful schemes or ones deliberately intended to startle, if not shock. What is certain is that they in no small measure serve to give a garden individuality, making each the personal creation of its owner.

In thinking about colour in the garden it is possibly helpful to consider the extent to which it is to become an integral part of all planning. Is a particular colour border to

In this garden the emphasis is clearly on summer colour.

Trees make real impact.

Gold and purple with two berberis.

Utterly restrained and totally charming.

The skill of the artist in this colour grouping.

Gardens need not be a riot of colour.

Quiet colours convey peace.

This simple trough is a mass of spring colour.

This display will remain looking good well into autumn.

These sweet peas form a colourful centrepiece.

be made in isolation, as a casual element within the garden, or is it to be planned as the main focus of a specific area? Is such a border to be viewed from all sides, as is the case with an island bed, or is it to be seen from one, or maybe two, angles only? Does the design allow for it to stand alone, or should it become paired? If not an island bed, then what is to form the background? All of these are questions which will need to be addressed before thoughts and ideas are finalized and work begins in earnest.

In positioning colours within the garden some account should be taken of external factors. The immediate surroundings are important for they will to a large extent determine how colours will appear. Boundaries, forming a background, will need to be in harmony with colours in adjacent borders. The brick of a house, or the paintwork around the windows, may well become determining influences in deciding what should be placed where. In an enclosed area, particularly where a single colour is to be used, what is viewed before and after may have a significant bearing on what plantings are chosen. Experimentation, a major part of the fun of gardening, will lead to what is appropriate and effective in each particular situation.

Colours of the Spectrum

The following pages provide a selection of plants divided into colour groups to help you plan schemes. Within each colour section, plants are listed chronologically from spring to autumn/winter.

Yellow and Cream

Yellow and cream are for many the colours of spring, and these shades are certainly not confined to members of the narcissus family. Flowering shrubs, like the familiar and much planted forsythia, or the less well known Chinese witch hazel, *Hamamelis × intermedia* 'Pallida', glow in the early sunlight. But, of course, yellow and cream do not belong to a single season. Whether through flower or on account of foliage used to lighten some gloomy corner, these are shades to enjoy all year long. However, what is true, and is possibly one of the reasons why pure yellow, as opposed to cream, remains somewhat unfashionable as a colour, is that it is not always the easiest colour to place. At all times it cries out for attention, seemingly advancing from its home in the border to meet and hold the eye. For this very reason it needs to be used with care lest it should upstage its companion plantings. Partially concealed from immediate view, to be happened upon as if by chance, a yellow border, or even a single golden foliaged shrub, may be relied upon to bring gaiety, movement and life to the dreariest of garden areas.

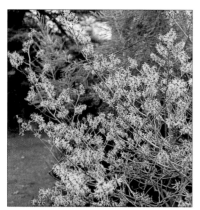

Hamamelis × intermedia 'Pallida'
Winter-flowering witch hazel is slow growing. 5 × 6m/16 × 20ft

Narcissus bulbocodium Tiny daffodil in late winter and early spring.
○, 15 × 20cm/6 × 8in

Primula veris Cowslips are to be found in damp meadows and glades. Equally at home in the garden, they may be used to brighten a spring border with their flowers. 20cm/8in

Primula auricula Pale lemon flowers cover this rockery primula each spring. 15 × 20cm/6 × 8in

Narcissus 'Hawera' An exciting, small flowered daffodil for springtime. 45cm/1.5ft

Caltha palustris Marsh marigolds contribute bold colour in spring. ◑, 30 × 45cm/1 × 1.5ft

Paeonia mlokosewitschii A spring-flowering perennial. Cultivate in humus-rich soil. 75 × 75cm/2.5 × 2.5ft

Meconopsis cambrica, the Welsh poppy, and *Euphorbia polychroma* are placed together at the base of shrubs in this colourful spring scene. The poppies will seed freely throughout a border.

Kerria japonica **'Pleniflora'** A vigorous shrub for spring. 2 × 2m/6 × 6ft

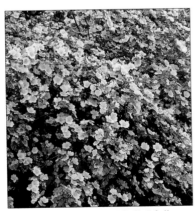

Rosa xanthina **'Canary Bird'** Of all shrub roses this is one of the earliest to flower. 2.2 × 2.2m/7 × 7ft

Erythronium **'Citronella'** Spring-flowering bulb for well drained soil in partial shade. ◖, 30 × 20cm/1ft × 8in

***Rosa* 'Frühlingsgold'** Butter-yellow, sweetly perfumed flowers clothe long, arching stems on this shrub rose during the late spring and the early summer. 2.2 × 2m/7 × 6ft

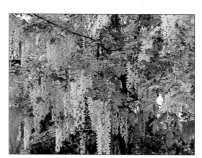

***Laburnum* × *watereri* 'Vossii'** Laburnum blooms in late spring. All parts are poisonous. 10 × 10m/33 × 33ft

Paeonia delavayi* var. *ludlowii Tree peonies are striking shrubs to include in any scheme. 2.4 × 2.4/8 × 8ft

Rhodiola rosea (*Sedum rhodiola*) A perennial for well drained soil in full sun. 20 × 30cm/8in × 1ft

Thermopsis montana As summer approaches this perennial begins to flower. 75 × 75cm/2.5 × 2.5ft

Early summer and this border is alive with interest. Lupins dominate, supported with butter-yellow irises. In the foreground a white achillea catches the eye.

Tanacetum (Chrysanthemum) parthenium **'Aureum'** The golden-leafed feverfew, with its aromatic leaves, is a short-lived perennial. 23 × 15cm/9 × 6in

Centaurea macrocephala Knapweed flowers in the early part of summer. 1m × 60cm/3 × 2ft

Cephalaria gigantea Flowers supported on tall stems appear at the start of summer. 2 × 1.2m/6 × 4ft

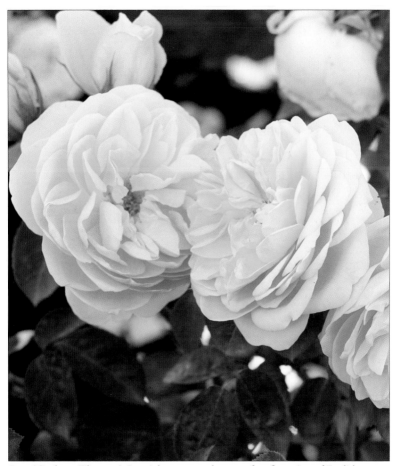

***Rosa* 'Graham Thomas'** Certainly amongst the most free flowering of English roses. Although the main time is early summer, 'Graham Thomas' will bloom for the entire season. 1.5 × 1.5m/5 × 5ft

***Lilium* 'Mont Blanc'** Summer-flowering lilies prefer their bulbs to be placed in free draining soil. For this reason they are ideal for pot cultivation. 1.2–2m/4–6ft

Inula magnifica An herbaceous perennial for the late summer. Placed at the back of the border these flowers are bound to make an impact. 2 × 1m/6 × 3ft

Santolina chamaecyparissus **'Lemon Queen'** A summer-flowering shrub with aromatic leaves and lemon flowers. Cut back hard in the spring to retain the shape.
○, E, 75cm × 1m/2.5 × 3ft

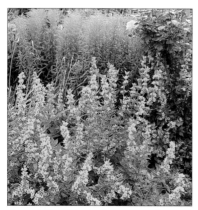

Brassy lysimachia, toning roses and swathes of golden rod in this yellow scheme.

Kniphofia **'Little Maid'** This summer poker is perennial. Delay cutting back until spring. 60 × 45cm/2 × 1.5ft

Potentilla fruticosa Shrubby potentillas flower for summer and often well into autumn. 1.2 × 1.2m/4 × 4ft

Genista aetnensis Midsummer and the Mount Etna broom is massed with flowers. 4 × 4m/13 × 13ft

Oenothera 'Fireworks' The flowers of this summer perennial are not easily ignored. This is a front of border plant for a situation where a noticeable colour is needed. ○, 45 × 30cm/1.5 × 1ft

A magnificent stand of yellow *Coreopsis verticillata* partnered with the slightly tender, velvety red *Cosmos atrosanguineus*.

Dahlia All of the dahlias prove themselves when late summer colour is the order of the day. From 30cm/1ft

***Helianthus* 'Monarch'** Tall growing perennials to flower at the end of summer. ◐, 2.1 × 1m/7 × 3ft

***Helenium* 'Golden Youth'** Perennials like this add colour to borders as the days of summer shorten. Divisions will guarantee free flowering plants. ◐, 1m × 60cm/3 × 2ft

***Helianthus* 'Lemon Queen'** All of these daisy-type perennials come into their own in late summer. ○, 2.1 × 1m/7 × 3ft

Oenothera missouriensis A form of the perennial evening primrose. In flower all summer. 20 × 60cm/8in × 2ft

***Rudbeckia fulgida* 'Goldsturm'** Autumn colour is captured in this late-flowering perennial which will continue to bloom for weeks on end. ○, 75 × 45cm/2.5 × 1.5ft

Euonymus fortunei **'Emerald 'n' Gold'**
Variegation on this small, cheerful shrub is effective throughout the year. E, 1 × 1m/ 3 × 3ft

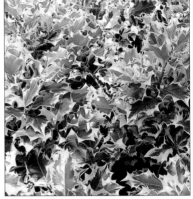

Ilex aquifolium **'Golden Queen'**
Possibly the most brilliant of all cultivars of common holly. A male variety.
E, 4 × 3m/13 × 10ft

Elaeagnus pungens **'Dicksonii'** This versatile shrub is most useful for providing year-round colour.
○, E, 2.4 × 3m/8 × 10ft

Choisya ternata **'Sundance'** This evergreen shrub carries perfumed white flowers in the spring. ○, E, 2 × 2m/ 6 × 6ft

Mahonia lomariifolia Wonderfully scented flowers in late autumn and early winter are a bonus with this shrub. Not totally hardy, it must be given the protection of a sunny wall. E, 3 × 2m/10 × 6ft

---

CONSIDER ALSO:

SHRUBS:
*Rhododendron
    luteum* (late
    spring)

ANNUALS:
Calendula
    (marigold)
Hibiscus trionum

PERENNIALS:
Primula florindae
    (summer)

BULBS:
Crocus chrysanthus
    'Cream Beauty'
    (spring)
Tulipa 'West Point'
    (late spring)

CLIMBERS:
Hedera helix
    'Buttercup'
    (golden foliage)

Jasminum nudiflorum Winter jasmine may be trained against walls. The flowers appear over winter. 2.4m/8ft

Orange

Poor orange, until recently a much despised colour among gardeners. Difficult to position with any certainty of success, this is a shade which has for a long time been relegated to the bottom of the heap. Yet this need not be so. For in banishing orange from a place in the border, there is a danger of ruling out of the garden many very worthy subjects.

Indeed, in today's climate where hot borders, the hotter the better, are not only acceptable but increasingly fashionable, orange is making a come-back. For the spirited, there is a case for clashing colours where one brilliant, vibrant shade is set against another. If nothing else, find a space for one of the wonderful acers, such as *Acer palmatum* 'Osakazuki', whose spectacular autumnal foliage is more than enough to set the world alight.

***Geum* 'Borisii'** Few flowers share the colour of this form of water avens. Throughout spring, and into early summer, this perennial will be alive with a succession of blooms. 45 × 45cm/1.5 × 1.5ft

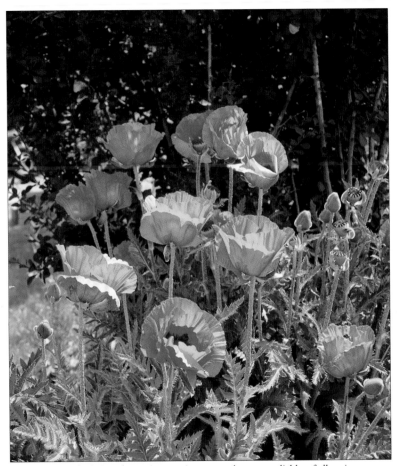

Papaver orientale Oriental poppies remain among the most reliable of all spring flowering perennials. By midsummer both foliage and flowers will have died down. 1m × 60cm/3 × 2ft

***Rosa* 'Schoolgirl'** Flowers cover this climbing rose during the early part of the summer. 3.5m/12ft

***Rosa* 'Iris Webb'** A floribunda rose producing pink blooms, with pale orange. 1.2 × 1m/4 × 3ft

***Rosa* 'Just Joey'** These blooms of creamy orange enlarge as the weather warms. 75 × 60cm/2.5 × 2ft

***Rosa* 'Anne Harkness'** Plant this healthy floribunda either singly or as a hedge. 1.2 × 1m/4 × 3ft

***Rosa* 'Sweet Dream'** Patio and miniature roses like this one need not be confined to the border. Free-flowering, they make excellent subjects for containers where they may be positioned for summer-long colour. 45cm/1.5ft

***Rosa* 'Brown Velvet'** Blooms are set off by foliage making this floribunda a flower arranger's dream. 75 × 60cm/2.5 × 2ft

***Rosa* 'Alchymist'** Midsummer sees this rose, which climbs, a mass of flowers. 3.5 × 2.4m/12 × 8ft

Digitalis parviflora A perennial foxglove for the first part of summer. For partial shade. 1m × 30cm/3 × 1ft

Hemerocallis **'Stafford'** Day lilies are summer-flowering perennials, unfussy about situation. 1m × 30cm/3 × 1ft

Tropaeolum tuberosum **'Ken Aslett'** A slightly tender climber which grows from a tuber which should, in cold areas, be lifted over winter. Flowers in summer. ○, 1.5m/5ft

Crocosmia masoniorum Still known as montbretia, this late summer perennial is noted for its flowers which hang from arching stems. Easy in both sun or partial shade. 60 × 30cm/2 × 1ft

Helenium 'Feuersiegel' End-of-season flowers for a late summer border. Perennial. 1m × 60cm/3 × 2ft

Crocosmia 'Harlequin' This gaily coloured montbretia will brighten autumnal borders. 60 × 30cm/2 × 1ft

Red

Red, so often thought of as a hot colour, is not necessarily so. On its cool side are to be found cerise pinks, shades of burgundy, crimson and deep, velvety maroons. They are reliable shades, holding their colour well in sunshine, and which appear jewel-like as the shadows lengthen towards the end of day. They give to the garden a feeling of tradition firmly rooted in an accessible past.

On the other hand, the vermilions and scarlets are to be found firmly among the hot reds. With their fiery brilliance they belong to late summer and autumn. Within the border they act as accents, advancing to arrest the eye, to advertise their somewhat strident gaiety. Within a large garden they may easily be accommodated. In a smaller area they should be used wisely and with care.

Camellia japonica **'Rubescens Major'** Camellias are shrubs for colour at the start of the year. They require acidic soil although they perform in conditions which are neutral. ○, E, 3 × 3m/10 × 10ft

Akebia quinata Slightly tender, the chocolate vine needs sun and protection. Scented flowers in the spring. 9m/30ft

***Tulipa greigii* 'Red Riding Hood'** Bulbs should be set out late autumn to flower the following year. 60 × 20cm/2ft × 8in

Rhododendron kaempferi Bursting with flower in the early spring, azaleas make an impact. All azaleas and rhododendrons are best suited to acidic soil and many benefit from leaf-mould.

Tulips like these with their unusual colouring give extra interest to the spring garden.

Euphorbia griffithii 'Fireglow' Orange bracts make this striking for early summer. 1m × 75cm/3 × 2.5ft

Paeonia arietina Peonies are lovely perennials with late spring and early summer flowers. 75 × 60cm/2.5 × 2ft

***Rosa moyesii* 'Geranium'** Early summer flowers followed in autumn with heps. 2.4 × 2.2m/8 × 7ft

***Acer palmatum* var. *dissectum* 'Garnet'** Splendid colour from beginning to end of the year. 1.5 × 2.4m/5 × 8ft

Tulipa sprengeri Virtually the last tulip to flower, this excites interest as late as early summer. ○, 45cm/1.5ft

Annual poppies bring random colour to borders where they seed around. Perennial oriental poppies, flowering at the start of summer, contribute a brief but dazzling show.

***Helianthemum* 'Supreme'** Rock roses are summer-flowering, for hot, well-drained sites. E, 30cm × 1m/1 × 3ft

***Lonicera* × *brownii* 'Dropmore Scarlet'** A vigorous climber for midsummer colour. 7m/23ft

***Clematis* 'Niobe'** Velvet flowers of this early summer clematis are especially appealing. This is a climber to grow over a shrub or into the lower branches of a small tree. 3m/10ft

***Paeonia lactiflora* 'Docteur H. Barnsby'** This peony adds a richness to the summer border. 60 × 60cm/2 × 2ft

***Clematis viticella* 'Madame Julia Correvon'** This clematis captures attention during late summer. 3m/10ft

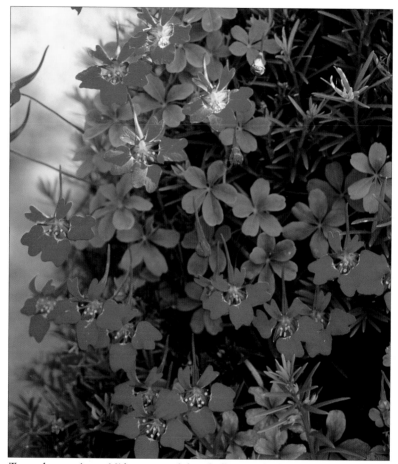

Tropaeolum speciosum Midsummer and these brilliant scarlet flowers abound. Position this climber against a dark background. In winter the plant is dormant. 2m/6ft

Rosa **'Baron Girod de l'Ain'** Old shrub rose which gives a border needed structure. 1.5 × 1.2m/5 × 4ft

Rosa **'Crimson Shower'** Flowers shower this rambling rose against the wall of a house. 6m/20ft

Rosa **'Hunter'** One of the rugosa roses which would serve as a hedge within the garden. It would make a background to a border planted in similar shades.
◗, 1.5 × 1.5m/5 × 5ft

Alcea Hollyhocks serve as a reminder of past cottage gardens. 2m × 60cm/6 × 2ft

Fuchsia **'Dollar Princess'** Hardy fuchsias give colour from summer to autumn. 75 × 75cm/2.5 × 2.5ft

Pelargonium **'Lord Bute'** A summer geranium; overwinter in a frost free greenhouse. ○, 45 × 45cm/1.5 × 1.5ft

***Penstemon* 'Red Knight'** Penstemons
flower, when deadheaded, until the frosts.
◑, E, 75 × 45cm/2.5 × 1.5ft

Lychnis chalcedonica These perennials
look good in summer when planted in a
mass. 1m × 45cm/3 × 1.5ft

***Crocosmia* 'Lucifer'** As summer draws to a close, 'Lucifer' is particularly effective.
1.2m × 30cm/4 × 1ft

Zinnia Sow seed in situ in the late spring in sun. Half-hardy annuals.
60cm–1m/2–3ft

Zauschneria californica Trumpets in later summer earn this perennial a place in a hot border. 60 × 60cm/2 × 2ft

***Dahlia* 'Bishop of Llandaff'** Grown from half-hardy tubers, which must be lifted over the winter, this dahlia is a favourite for the end of summer and into autumn.
1m × 60cm/3 × 2ft

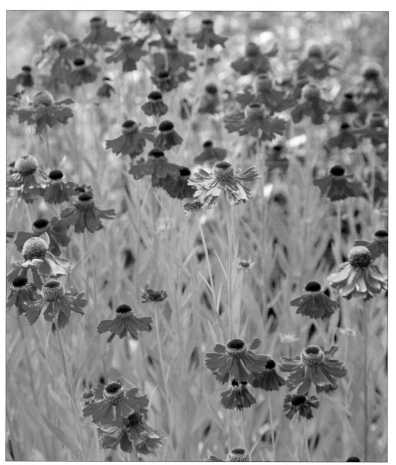

***Helenium* 'Moerheim Beauty'** Not strictly red as such, this perennial associates
perfectly with so many other colours. ○, 1m × 60cm/3 × 2ft

Salvia splendens This tender annual has a place in bedding schemes. ○, 30 × 30cm/ 1 × 1ft

Lobelia 'Compliment' Late summer perennial. Cover in winter. ○, 1.2m × 30cm/4 × 1ft

Tropaeolum majus This scrambling nasturtium is easily raised each year from seed. ○, 30 × 30cm/1 × 1ft

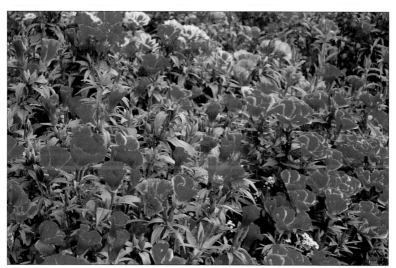

Godetia A hardy annual to liven up the summer borders or to include in pots and containers. Seed of godetia may be bought in mixed packets. 25–75cm/10in–2.5ft

Amaranthus caudatus Love-lies-bleeding is one of the most versatile of all annuals. 1.2m/4ft

***Hibiscus syriacus* 'Woodbridge'** Flowers cover this shrub in late summer. ○, 2 × 2m/6 × 6ft

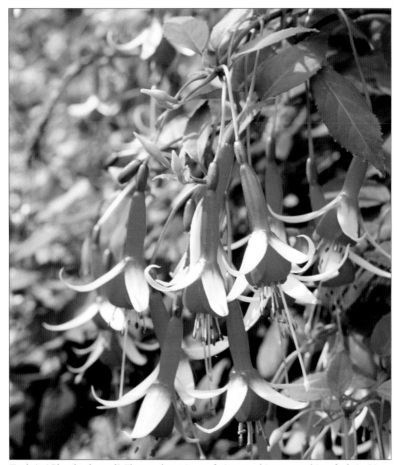

Fuchsia **'Checkerboard'** Flowers hang in profusion on this eye-catching fuchsia. Use within the border or display in tubs for seasonal colour. 75 × 75cm/2.5 × 2.5ft

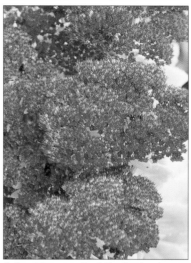

***Sedum* 'Autumn Joy'** Flat heads of flowers remain attractive well into winter. ◯, 60 × 60cm/2 × 2ft

Schizostylis coccinea A perennial for moist soil. These flowers appear at the last. 60 × 30cm/2 × 1ft

CONSIDER ALSO:

SHRUBS:
Chaemomeles 'Crimson and Gold' (spring)
Rosa 'Scarlet Fire' (summer)

PERENNIALS:
Dianthus 'Gravetye Gem' (summer)
Iris sibirica 'Helen Astor' (summer)

ANNUALS:
Eschscholzia 'Cherry Ripe'
Papaver commutatum 'Lady Bird'

BULBS:
Anemone fulgens (spring)
Tulipa 'Queen of Sheba' (spring)

***Berberis thunbergii* 'Rose Glow'** The attraction of this easy shrub is the colour of the leaves. 1.5 × 1.5m/5 × 5ft

Pinks and Pastels

These are the very essence of the traditional garden with its arbours of old-fashioned roses, paths lined with lavenders, sweetly scented stocks and borders brimming with old-time favourites. All of the lovely pinks, and their associated colours of lilac, pale mauve, washed out purple, rosy red and white streaked with blue, contribute to this.

In early spring, when frosts still play havoc, wonderful camellias come into their own, their dark glossy leaves showing off waxy blooms. Then, too, the daphnes are in flower, their fragrance filling the entire garden. Later the magnolias, cherries in blossom, and early flowering clematis. By summer there are roses, with all their companion plantings, irises, pinks and mallows, lilies and lovely, tender annuals. As warm days ebb away, and autumn approaches, Japanese anemones vie with muted asters to put on a late show.

Camellia **'Galaxie'** Camellias are shrubs of the early spring. Plant where they thrive in leaf-mould in acidic or neutral soil. ◯, E, 2 × 2m/6 × 6ft

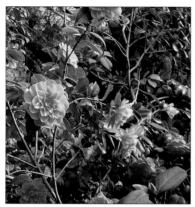

Camellia **'Water Lily'** In spring sugar-pink blooms cover this shrub.
◑, E, 2 × 2m/6 × 6ft

Prunus cerasifera **'Nigra'** Flowers festoon this tree in spring. 4.5 × 4.5m/15 × 15ft

Magnolia × *soulangeana* **'Lennei'** A spreading tree producing flowers in spring. ◑, 3 × 3m/10 × 10ft

Clematis macropetala **'Markham's Pink'** Early flowering climber which can be left to its own devices to weave a passage among other springtime plantings. 1.8m/6ft

Clematis alpina **'Willy'** Seen with *Geranium macrorrhizum*, this climber is a delight in spring. 2.4m/8ft

Clematis **'Nelly Moser'** Flowering in the spring, 'Nelly Moser' never loses popularity. ◯, 2.4m/8ft

Malus × moerlandsii **'Profusion'** Flowering crab-apples are lovely in springtime. Later there will be deep red fruits. 4.5 × 4.5m/15 × 15ft

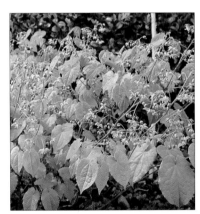

Epimedium × youngianum **'Roseum'** Cut foliage back before spring flowers of this perennial emerge. 25 × 30cm/ 10in × 1ft

Scilla non-scripta Pink bluebells make a welcome change in spring. ○, 25cm/10in

***Prunus tenella* 'Firehill'** Flowers in spring extend along the branches of this shrub. ◑, 2 × 2m/6 × 6ft

***Paeonia suffruticosa* 'Sitifukujin'** This tree peony carries its fine flowers in the spring. ◑, 2.2 × 2.2m/7 × 7ft

***Daphne* × *burkwoodii* 'Somerset'** Heavily scented, spring flowering daphnes really do have to be included if at all possible. Slow growing, they are not difficult to accommodate. ◑, Semi-E, 1.5 × 1m/5 × 3ft

Paeonia lactiflora **'Monsieur Jules Elie'**
The large, slightly blowzy heads belong to
the early summer. 1 × 1m/3 × 3ft

Incarvillea delavayi This is an early
summer perennial for rich soil in full sun.
☽, 60 × 30cm/2 × 1ft

Deutzia × *elegantissima* **'Rosealind'** Tiny flowers are massed together on this shrub
which blooms from the late spring into the early summer. 1 × 1.5m/3 × 5ft

***Tulipa* 'China Pink'** Plant bulbs deeply
in autumn with a dozen or more to each
planting hole. 45cm/1.5ft

***Rosa* 'May Queen'** Blooms appear on
this rambling rose in summer. 5m/15ft

Primula vialii A summer-flowering
perennial for moist soil. 30 × 30cm/
1 × 1ft

***Rosa* 'Pink Elizabeth Arden'** Furnish large mixed borders at the start of summer
with shrub roses such as this one. Feed generously. 1.5 × 1.5m/5 × 5ft

***Chaerophyllum hirsutum* 'Roseum'** This
perennial is like a pink cow parsley.
60 × 60cm/2 × 2ft

***Prunella grandiflora* 'Pink Loveliness'**
Flowers cover this perennial for many
weeks in the summertime.
30 × 30cm/1ft × 1ft

Penstemon venustus A penstemon for
early summer. Give good drainage and
sun. 45 × 45cm/1.5 × 1.5ft

***Geranium cinereum* 'Ballerina'** A neat
plant. After the summer flowers the leaves
remain pretty. 20 × 30cm/8in × 1ft

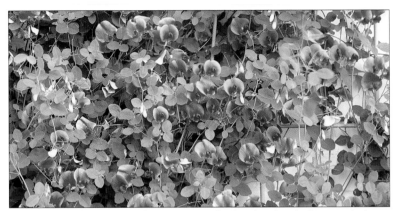

Lathyrus grandiflorus Shades of magenta are to be found in this climbing, everlasting pea. Vigorous, it will put on enough growth in one season to cover a fence. ◯, 1.5m/5ft

***Clematis viticella* 'Margot Koster'** In bloom for the summer, a good climber. 3m/10ft

Papaver rhoeas An annual. This variety is a double form. 45cm/1.5ft

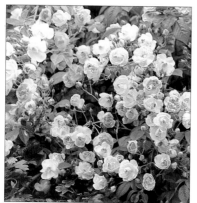

Rosa **'Princess Marie'** Large, rambling roses may be used to climb into trees. 4.5m/15ft

Rosa **'Raubritter'** Clusters of flowers in summer. 1 × 1.5/3 × 5ft

Rosa **'Albertine'** Rambling rose suitable for growing over a pergola. 5.4m/18ft

Oxalis articulata Enjoy these flowers from the late spring onwards. A low growing, easily cultivated perennial which will tolerate dry shade. 20 × 20cm/8 × 8in

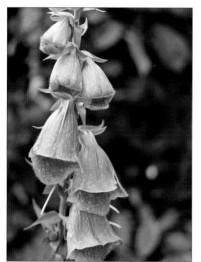

Digitalis* × *mertonensis Perennial flowers in summer on this foxglove. 1m × 60cm/ 3 × 2ft

***Phlox paniculata* 'Fairy's Petticoat'** Border phloxes are one of the mainstays of summer. 75 × 60cm/2.5 × 2ft

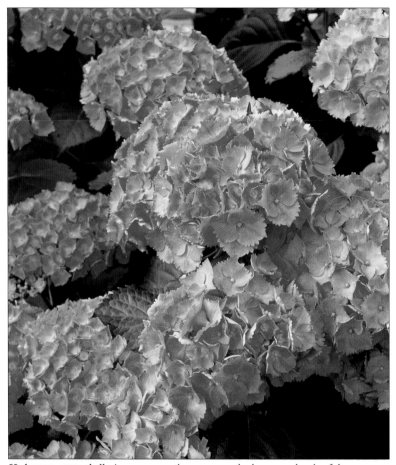

Hydrangea macrophylla As summer gathers pace, so the large mopheads of the hydrangeas come into their own. Colour will always vary according to soil type. Hydrangeas are also ideal subjects for tubs or large containers. 2 × 2.4m/6 × 8ft

Hydrangea macrophylla **'Ayesha'** The flowers of this hydrangea are unique for the way in which the petals are curved. For best results choose a place in the garden which is slightly shaded. 1 × 1.5m/3 × 5ft

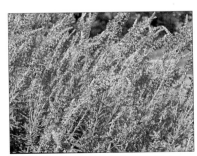

Lythrum salicaria Purple loosestrife is suited to damp conditions. Easy in sun or part shade. 1m × 30cm/3 × 1ft

Clematis texensis **'Princess of Wales'** A late flowering clematis. Hard prune in early spring. 3m/10ft

Echinacea purpurea Perennials to include in the late summer border. 1.2m × 60cm/ 4 × 2ft

Fuchsia **'Garden News'** Hardy fuchsias bring colour which continues until frosts. 60 × 60cm/2 × 2ft

Oenothera speciosa **'Pink Petticoats'** A pale pink form of the evening primrose to spread at the front of a border. Preferring a sunny spot, it should flower throughout summer. 15 × 60cm/6in × 2ft

Lobelia × speciosa hybrid Rich soil, not allowed to dry out, for this summer perennial. 75 × 45cm/2.5 × 1.5ft

Lilium speciosum var. rubrum A fragrant Japanese lily which flowers in late summer. 1.5m/5ft

Crinum × powellii A bulb sporting trumpet-shaped flowers. To succeed, plant in a hot position in full sun and in soil which is free-draining. ◖, 1m × 60cm/3 × 2ft

Schizostylis coccinea **'Sunrise'** Enjoy these late flowering perennials in the autumn. 60 × 30cm/2 × 1ft

Gypsophila **'Rosy Veil'** All gypsophilas are summer perennials. This one forms a low mat. 20 × 30cm/8in × 1ft

Nerine bowdenii These autumn flowering bulbs hail from South Africa so are, understandably, in need of a site where they may enjoy as much sunshine as possible. ◯, 45 × 20cm/1.5ft × 8in

***Aster novi–belgii* 'Goliath'** Autumn Michaelmas daisies bring life to the garden as days shorten. 'Goliath', planted in sun, will reward for several weeks with these pink flowers with their bold yellow centres. ◐, 1.2m × 45cm/4 × 1.5ft

Colchicum speciosum Dwarf flowering bulbs for the autumn assist in extending the season. The large basal leaves appear after the flowers in late winter or early spring. ◐, 20 × 20cm/8 × 8in

Cleome spinosa The spider flower is an annual which deserves more widespread cultivation. 1m/3ft

***Verbena* 'Aveyron'** A perennial verbena for end-of-season colour. Plants like this need to be massed together. 60 × 30cm/ 2 × 1ft

Arbutus unedo* f. *rubra If your soil is inclined towards the acidic, then try this splendid form of the strawberry tree. Strangely, it flowers in the autumn at the same time as its fruits begin to ripen. E, 5 × 5m/16 × 16ft

Physostegia virginiana This late summer perennial is ideal for planting between shrubs where it will spread to form an effective and decorative form of ground cover. Once the flowers are over, the whole plant may be cut down to ground level. 30 × 30cm/ 1 × 1ft

CONSIDER ALSO:

SHRUBS:
*Kolkwitzia
   amabilis* 'Pink
   Cloud'
   (summer)
*Rhododendron
   yakushimanum*
   (spring)
Viburnum ×
   bodnantense
   'Dawn'
   (autumn–
   winter)

ANNUALS:
Cosmos
   'Daydream'

PERENNIALS:
Anemone × *hybrida*
   'Queen
   Charlotte' (late
   summer–
   autumn)
Phlox 'Mother of
   Pearl' (summer–
   autumn)

BULBS:
Anemone blanda
   'Pink Star'
   (spring)
Lilium 'Pink
   Perfection'
   (summer)

Amaryllis belladonna Late-flowering perfumed bulb. Plant deeply in a sheltered position. ○, 75cm/2.5ft

Purple and Lilac

Of all colours, these are possibly amongst the most moody, often associated, together with black, as the colours of mourning. However, by widening the range to include some shades of lavender, magenta and the darkest of ruby reds, then some exciting variations are realized.

Bearing in mind the potential for creating totally deadening effects, then purple is most certainly not a colour for shade. Where possible such hues are best viewed back-lit, that is to say with the sun shining through them from behind. When this occurs, both foliage and flower adopt a magical quality that surprises as much as it delights. If at all possible, then try to contrive such an area within a much frequented part of the garden. Whatever, avoid placing close to the boundaries of a country garden for this is a colour which does not associate well with green fields.

Crocus tommasinianus Early spring colour develops with these tiny bulbs. Left undisturbed, they will gradually increase with time. 10cm/4in

Pulsatilla vulgaris Rich purple, spring flowers on this perennial plant. The Pasque flower is suitable either for the rock garden or scree bed, or for the front of the border. 30 × 30cm/1 × 1ft

Fritillaria meleagris A spring bulb which is at home growing in grass. Allow to seed. ○, 25cm/10in

Rhododendron augustinii This shrub is massed each spring with flowers. ○, E, 3 × 3m/10 × 10ft

***Aquilegia vulgaris* 'Adelaide Addison'**
Allow these spring and early summer
perennials to seed around. ◯, 75 × 45cm/
2.5 × 1.5ft

Nepeta mussinii Catmints are hardy. Cut
back when the early summer flowers are
over. 45 × 75cm/1.5 × 2.5ft

***Tulipa* 'Blue Heron'** Flowering in the late spring, this wonderful violet-purple tulip
has crystal-like fringes all around the top of the petals, rather like miniature, frosted
icicles. ◯, 60cm/2ft

***Clematis* 'Proteus'** Blooms of a delicate mauve-pink. The main flowering period is in the first part of the summer. However, it will produce a reasonable second show at the approach of autumn. 2m/6ft

Abutilon suntense Late spring onwards sees this shrub in flower. Slightly tender. ◯, 5 × 3m/15 × 10ft

Wisteria floribunda One of the sights of early summer are the long racemes of a well-grown wisteria. ◯, 9m/30ft

***Clematis* 'Haku-ôkan'** This climber blooms towards the end of spring. 2m/6ft

Within this garden a sunny slope has been used with great imagination and artistry. Different creeping thymes, with an emphasis on dark purple, have been arranged to resemble an antique rug thrown carelessly to one side.

Trifolium rubens An unusual perennial with flower heads in the early summer. 30 × 30cm/1 × 1ft

Malva sylvestris mauritiana Flowers appear on this perennial from spring until autumn. ◯, 1.2m × 60cm/4 × 2ft

Allium aflatunense **'Purple Sensation'**
Combine this tall-growing bulb with
purple bearded irises for springtime
colour. 1m/3ft

Iris **'Mandarin'** In this planting it looks
fine in early summer against the
euphorbia. 1m × 30cm/3 × 1ft

Penstemon glaber All of the penstemons will repay dead-heading. To extend the season,
select *Penstemon* 'Papal Purple', 'Blackbird' and 'Catherine de la Mare'.
○, E, 60 × 60cm/2 × 2ft

***Rosa* 'Zigeunerknabe'** ('Gipsy Boy')
Summer-flowering roses are wonderful
shrubs. 1.5 × 1.2m/5 × 4ft

***Rosa* 'Bleu Magenta'** Clusters of blooms
cling to the stems of this climbing rose.
4.5m/15ft

***Rosa* 'Blue Boy'** Place this shrub rose as the centrepiece of a border devoted to shades
of crimson, magenta, deep pink and violet for an exciting and out of the ordinary
picture. 1 × 1m/3 × 3ft

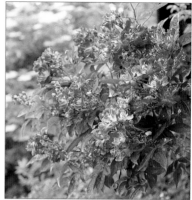

Phlox **'Chattahoochee'** For spring colour, plant this perennial phlox in a sunny spot. 20 × 30cm/8in × 1ft

Rosa **'Veilchenblau'** A rose to climb over a pergola or a wall. 3.5m/12ft

Erigeron speciosus **'Pink Jewel'** This lilac-pink daisy with a centre of old gold will be in flower each year all through the summer. 75 × 30cm/2.5 × 1ft

Salvia sclarea* var. *turkestanica Faded purple bracts appear from midsummer on this biennial sage. 75 × 30cm/2.5 × 1ft

Acanthus spinosissimus A perennial with flowers in midsummer. ○, 1.2 × 75cm/ 4 × 2.5ft

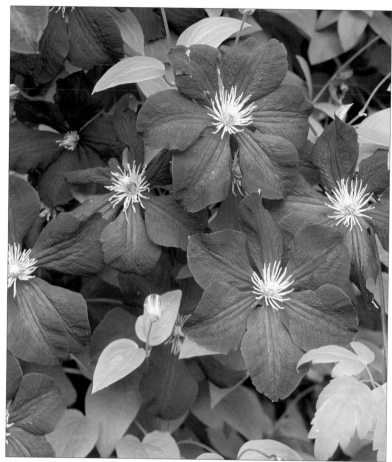

***Clematis viticella* 'Etoile Violette'** Flowers first appear in midsummer and continue well into autumn. Viticella clematis are pruned in the late winter to ground level. 3m/10ft

Aster frikartii **'Mönch'** Summer-flowering Michaelmas daisy. It blooms for months on end. ◯, 75 × 45cm/2.5 × 1.5ft

Verbena bonariensis Grow this short-lived perennial at the front of the border from midsummer onwards. 1.2m × 15cm/4ft × 6in

Allium sphaerocephalon Known as the round-headed leek, these bulbs may be used to grow up through other summer plantings. Plant in sufficient numbers to look purposeful. 30–60cm/1–2ft

Passiflora caerulea The common name for this summer climber is the passion flower. It is probably the hardiest. ◗, 6m/20ft

***Geranium clarkei* 'Kashmir Purple'** Perennial hardy geranium. This flowers in summer. 30 × 30cm/1 × 1ft

This section of a late summer border brings together shrubs and perennials of similar tones. Plants featuring here are *Hydrangea aspera* Villosa Group, a border phlox and the flat heads of *Achillea millefolium* 'Lilac Beauty'.

Lavenders possess an old-fashioned quality. As illustrated here, they may be planted together to join up as an informal, but colourful and scented hedge.

***Buddleja davidii* 'Dartmoor'** Flower spikes appear on the current growth of this shrub towards the end of summer. 3 × 3m/10 × 10ft

Gladiolus papilio This is in flower as summer ends. 1m/3ft

Salvia horminum Grow this form of annual clary for its dark violet bracts in summertime. An excellent plant for flower arrangers. 45cm/1.5ft

Eupatorium purpureum A tall perennial for the end of summer. Place in moist soil. 2 × 1m/6 × 3ft

Clematis viticella **'Purpurea Plena Elegans'** With double blooms, this is a climber for late summer and early autumn. 3.5m/12ft

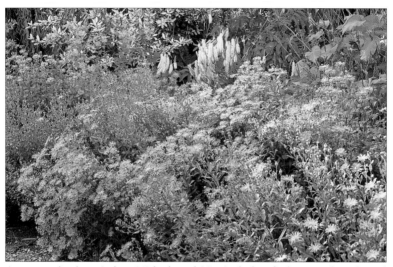

An autumn border at its best. Michaelmas daisies, in shades of pale mauve, lavender and lilac, are grouped together in this garden to give a misty effect.

CONSIDER ALSO:

SHRUBS:
Buddleja davidii
  'Black Knight'
  (late summer)
Syringa 'Elinor'
  (early summer)

PERENNIALS:
Geranium
  magnificum
  (summer)
Liriope muscari
  (autumn)

ANNUALS:
Heliotropium
  'Marine'
Petunia 'Plum
  Purple'

BULBS:
Iris reticulata
  (spring)
Tulipa 'First Lady'

Clematis **'Gypsy Queen'** Plum-purple flowers appear on this climber from the middle of summer until autumn. 3m/10ft

Blue

Blue remains one of the most covetable of all colours within the garden. Perhaps this is in no small measure because of its shy, retiring habit. Unassertive, it is one of the last colours to declare itself in the early morning and, as the dusk gathers, the first to fade from prominence. Because of this it is useful for creating a sense of distance, for conveying the impression that a border, or indeed garden, is actually rather longer than it in fact is.

Blue used singly may well appear a little dull, lifeless and lack-lustre. It is a colour to be partnered with others in a deliberately thought out scheme, or to be a token, a mere suggestion, within a mixed colour border.

Lithodora diffusa Poor, stony, lime-free soil is the ideal medium in which to grow this shrub which will produce flowers for the greater part of the summer. 30 × 60cm/ 1 × 2ft

Scilla mischtschenkoana Early squills enjoy a situation not too hot. 10cm/4in

Chionodoxa luciliae Glory of the Snow bulbs flower at the start of the spring. 10cm/4in

Clematis **'Blue Bird'** Choose early spring flowering clematis for colour at the start of the year. All of the alpina types look effective trained to grow through a shrub. 1.8–2.4m/6–8ft

Gentiana acaulis For the spring rock garden. ◑, E, 10 × 15cm/4 × 6in

Corydalis flexuosa Flowers in the springtime. Position in semi-shade. 30 × 30cm/1 × 1ft

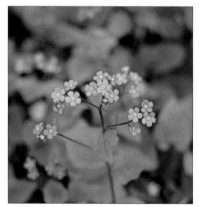

Brunnera macrophylla The Siberian bugloss makes excellent ground cover in the spring garden. ◑, 45 × 60cm/ 1.5 × 2ft

Muscari aucheri This grape hyacinth will provide vivid colour each spring. 10–15cm/4–6in

Veronica pinnata **'Blue Eyes'** Plant this summer-flowering perennial at the front of a border. ◐, 20 × 30cm/8in × 1ft

Veronica teucrium **'Shirley Blue'** This perennial flowers profusely throughout the summer. 20 × 30cm/8in × 1ft

Iris missouriensis This iris will thrive with blooms in early summer. 60 × 60cm/ 2 × 2ft

Iris sibirica **'Soft Blue'** Border plants for the late spring into the first part of summer. 80 × 60cm/2.5 × 2ft

Rosmarinus officinalis Common rosemary need not be confined to the herb garden. ○, E, 1.5 × 1.5m/5 × 5ft

Ceanothus impressus Grow this shrub for its deep blue flowers each springtime. ○, E, 1.5 × 3m/5 × 10ft

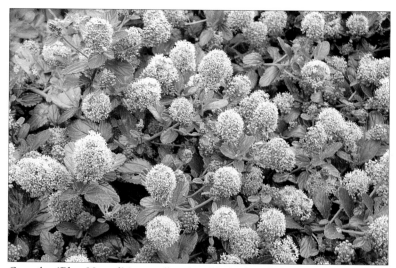

***Ceanothus* 'Blue Mound'** In a small garden, this shrub is ideal. The flowers appear from late spring. All ceanothus benefit from shelter and good drainage. ○, E, 30 × 60cm/1 × 2ft

Camassia leichtlinii Flowers rise out of lush foliage in early summer. 75 × 30cm/ 2.5 × 1ft

Campanula latiloba Spires of blue bring a vibrancy to summer borders. 60 × 60cm/ 2 × 2ft

Delphinium belladonna **'Lamartine'** Perennial delphiniums are one of the mainstays of the garden in the summer. Tall stems, which may require staking, give height to borders. 1.5m × 60cm/5 × 2ft

Felicia amelloides A tender perennial best treated as an annual. Flowers throughout summer. Grow them also in pots and containers. ○, 45 × 45cm/1.5 × 1.5ft

Clematis durandii Flowers from midsummer until autumn. 1–1.2m/3–4ft

Anchusa azurea '**Loddon Royalist**' True blue for the first part of summer. 1.2 × 60cm/4 × 2ft

Campanula latifolia Flowers mass this perennial in summer. 1m × 60cm/3 × 2ft

Campanula cochleariifolia A mat of bells in midsummer. 10 × 60cm/4in × 2ft

Salvia patens A summer-flowering perennial. This is not hardy. 60 × 45cm/2 × 1.5ft

Hydrangea macrophylla **'Blue Wave'** Late summer flowering shrub. The exact colour depends on the soil. The greater the acidity, the more intense the blue. 2 × 2.7m/ 6 × 9ft

Hydrangeas add flamboyancy to end of summer borders.

Ceanothus **'Autumnal Blue'** A late summer flowering shrub amongst the hardiest of ceanothus. ○, E, 4 × 4m/ 13 × 13ft

Platycodon grandiflorus mariesii Open panned flowers line the stems of this perennial in summer. The balloon flower will tolerate most situations apart from complete shade. 60 × 45cm/2 × 1.5ft

Allium beesianum One of the onion family, this bulbous plant flowers in summer. 45cm/1.5ft

***Agapanthus* Headbourne Hybrids** Flowerheads in summer. Bulbs are exceedingly hardy. ○, 60 × 45cm/ 2 × 1.5ft

Ceratostigma plumbaginoides The hardy plumbago is one of the loveliest of shrubs for its flowers in early autumn. Position where it will catch the sun in dry, well drained soil. 1 × 1.5m/3 × 5ft

Perovskia atriplicifolia Russian sage is a shrub to enjoy in later summer.
1 × 1.5m/3 × 5ft

Nicandra physalodes The shoo-fly, a hardy annual, flowers in late summer.
1–1.2m/3–4ft

Caryopteris* × *clandonensis This small shrub is valued for its late flowers over glaucous leaves. ○, 80 × 80cm/2.5 × 2.5ft

***Picea pungens* 'Koster'** The leaves of this pine are silvery-blue, spectacular during winter. E, 13 × 8m/43 × 26ft

CONSIDER ALSO:

SHRUBS:
Hibiscus syriacus
  'Bluebird' (late
  summer)

ANNUALS:
Nigella damascena
  (Love-in-a-
  mist)
Phacelia
  campanularia

PERENNIALS:
Pulmonaria
  angustifolia
  'Munstead
  Blue' (spring)
Salvia uliginosa
  (autumn)

BULBS:
Muscari neglectum
  (spring)
Scilla sibirica
  'Spring Beauty'

Ilex meservae The blue holly takes its name from its blue foliage. E, 3 × 2.4m/ 10 × 8ft

Green

Of all the colours in the garden green is, for some extraordinary reason, the least valued. Featuring so often, and in so many guises, its true worth has almost completely become overlooked. Yet green is the most restful of colours which, acting as a foil to others, brings order, harmony and certain restraint to even the most restless of schemes.

That apart, it brings with it wonderful variation of form and texture to be found in both leaf and flower alike. For green encompasses so much. It is the colour of so many grasses, of ferns, of sedges and bamboos, of trees and shrubs unfurling new, precious shoots in the early spring as well as the bold sentinels of evergreens dominating the winter landscape. Green flowers give a subtlety to borders for they are understated and often, delightfully, unexpected.

Formal, structured gardens, where flowers may appear inappropriate, depend almost in their entirety on form provided by such plants as clipped box, yew, Portuguese laurel (*Prunus lusitanica*), hollies and ivies as well, of course, as grass with which to set off the whole effect.

This corner of a terrace relies heavily on green plants, both for their form and texture, to create an effect which is restful yet is not without interest.

Garrya elliptica Shrub noted for catkins in winter, best on male plants. E, 4 × 3m/ 13 × 10ft

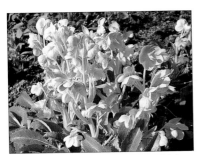

Helleborus argutifolius This perennial is a delight in the early year. E, 60 × 90cm/ 2 × 3ft

Euphorbia characias **ssp. *wulfenii* 'Lambrook Gold'** This fine form of spurge flowers in spring. 1.2m × 1m/ 4 × 3ft

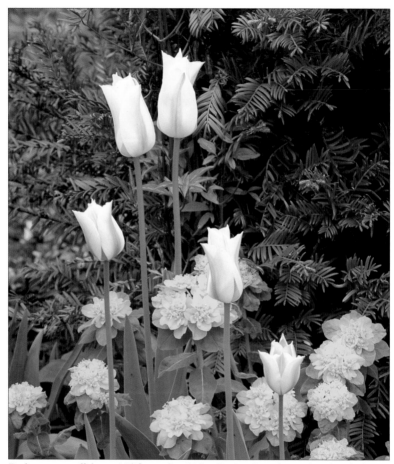

Dark yew sets off these viridiflora tulips, *Tulipa* 'Spring Green'. Combined with these is *Euphorbia polychroma*, its bracts complementing the colour of the tulips.

An unusual use of fennel, its foliage contrasted with the eryngium.

This composition is principally made up of *Heuchera* 'Greenfinch', *Iris pseudacorus* and *Rheum alexandrae*.

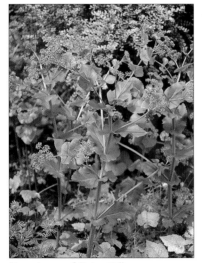

Smyrnium perfoliatum Yellow-green flowers of this summer perennial give scope to gardeners. 1m × 60cm/3 × 2ft

Euphorbia* × *martinii A spurge with flower spikes from early summer. ◐, 60 × 30cm/2 × 1ft

Bupleurum angulosum A much admired
perennial for its flowers. Place in sun.
60 × 30cm/2 × 1ft

Seedheads of crown imperials extend the
period of interest of these bulbous plants.

These mixed conifers are highlighted by a broad sweep of lady's mantle which
produces lime-green flowers throughout the summer months. *Alchemilla mollis* self-
seeds freely. 45 × 45cm/1.5 × 1.5ft

Stipa tenuissima This perennial grass looks pleasing in late summer when it flowers. ○, 60 × 45cm/2 × 1.5ft

Euphorbia sikkimensis A foliage plant with lime bracts for weeks in summer. 1m × 75cm/3 × 2½ft

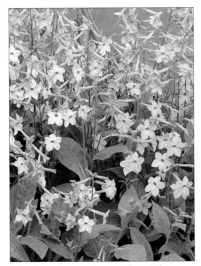

Nicotiana Green tobacco plants. This annual is not completely hardy. 1m × 30cm/3 × 1ft

Eucomis bicolor A bulb for a warm position. Spires in late summer. ○, 45 × 60cm/1.5 × 2ft

Adiantum venustum Plant the deciduous maidenhair fern to enjoy its delicate foliage. 25 × 25cm/10 × 10in

***Polystichum setiferum* 'Divisilobum'** The shield fern is evergreen. E, 1.2m × 1m/ 4 × 3ft

Veratrum nigrum Leaves of this perennial open out as variegated surfaces. Late summer flowers. 1.5m × 60cm/5 × 2ft

Laurus nobilis Bay may be grown as a handsome, evergreen shrub. ◯, 7 × 2m/23 × 6ft

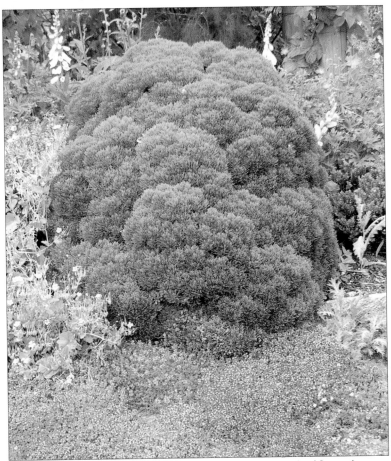

***Hebe cupressoides* 'Boughton Dome'** This hebe makes up for lack of flowers by being evergreen and shapely. Placed within a border it contributes year-round form. 75 × 75cm/2.5 × 2.5ft

***Miscanthus* 'Silver Feather'** Glossy green leaves, with variegation, are followed with plumes. 2m × 60cm/6 × 2ft

Pseudosasa japonica Evergreen bamboo, which produces a thicket of canes. 5m/15ft indefinite spread

Phormium tenax The evergreen phormium is dramatic. During cold winters it may prove wise to protect with old sacking. 3 × 1m/10 × 3ft

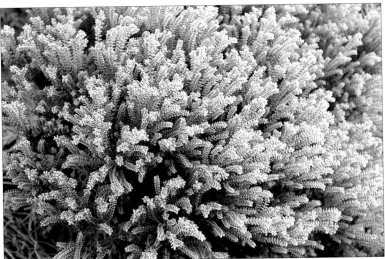

Hebe × *divergens* **'Edinensis'** The architectural quality of this evergreen shrub should not be overlooked. In this picture it has been caught heavily laden with frost.
30cm × 1m/1 × 3ft

Salvia officinalis Evergreen, shrubby sage with its aromatic leaves. For sun.
1 × 1m/3 × 3ft

Tanacetum vulgare The leaves of this tansy make it highly decorative. 1m × 60cm/3 × 2ft

Variegation

Variegation in plants, usually to be found in foliage, provides an element of variety within the garden and is popular with gardeners very often as a means of brightening some otherwise gloomy or dark corner. Brought about by a chlorophyll deficiency in the main, variegated plants have in recent times been avidly collected by enthusiasts. If there is any danger in this, then it lies in over-planting. Much greater harmony overall will be found where plants with variegation are used sparingly, perhaps singly, or as part of a carefully thought out, colour-themed border.

All combinations are inclined from time to time to revert to plain green. Where individual leaves, or even whole stems or branches, do revert, then these should be cut out immediately they are first spotted.

Weigela florida **'Variegata'** This shrub appears fresh on account of its foliage. Arching branches of flowers in early summer make it ideal. 1.5 × 1.5/5 × 5ft

Euonymus fortunei **'Silver Queen'** This has crisp leaves which are evergreen. E, 2.4 × 1.5m/8 × 5ft

Euonymus fortunei **'Emerald 'n' Gold'** Much of the popularity of this shrub has to be on account of its foliage. E, 1 × 1.5m/3 × 5ft

Cornus alba **'Elegantissima'** This red-barked dogwood may be used to lighten a dull spot or as a basis for an all white scheme. 3 × 4m/10 × 13ft

Ilex aquifolium **'Argentea Marginata Pendula'** Hollies are useful for providing out-of-season colour. E, 2.4 × 2.4m/ 8 × 8ft

Leucothoe walteri **'Rainbow'** A shrub with pink, variegated leaves. 75cm × 1m/ 2.5 × 3ft

Aralia elata **'Variegata'** Japanese angelica tree merits a warm situation where new foliage won't be frosted. In late summer it is massed with white flowers. 3.5 × 3m/12 × 10ft

Aucuba japonica **'Gold Dust'** Aucubas may be relied upon to thrive in difficult situations. E, 2.4 × 2.4m/8 × 8ft

Lonicera japonica **'Aureoreticulata'** The attraction of this honeysuckle is its leaves. 3m/10ft

Acer negundo **'Flamingo'** The appeal of this deciduous tree has to be the variegation of the leaves. Distinctly marked white, green and pink they create a display. 8 × 6m/26 × 20ft

Hosta **'Frances Williams'** Lime-green is matched in equal parts with grey-green for an unusual combination. 75 × 75cm/ 2.5 × 2.5ft

Hedera colchica **'Sulphur Heart'** Bold splashes of gold colour the vibrant green of this evergreen, climbing ivy. E, 4.5m/15ft

Brunnera macrophylla **'Dawson's White'** In maturity these spring-flowering perennials make an excellent plant. ○, 45 × 60cm/1.5 × 2ft

Hedera helix **'Goldheart'** This evergreen favourite ivy really is alight with colour throughout the year. E, 9m/30ft

Houttuynia cordata **'Chameleon'** This showy, ground-cover perennial is all too often overlooked as an interesting plant for the garden. It makes a lovely addition to the water garden where it enjoys moisture retentive soil. ○, 10cm/4in, indefinite spread

Thymus **'Doone Valley'** Tiny aromatic flowers and leaves have made thyme an enduring plant. 10cm/4in

Spartina pectinata **'Aureomarginata'** Plant close to water with room to spread as it can prove to be invasive. 1.8m/6ft

White, Grey and Black

Gardening in this range makes its own demands, but white flowers and grey leaves, for example, are vital components of the plantsman's palette, though black tends to be more of a sought-after oddity.

White

White, the symbol of purity, innocence and perfection continues, more than any other colour in the garden, to hold the position of utmost supremacy. White flowers in absolute plenty carry with them a richness married with, paradoxically, a quiet, gentle sophistication.

To be totally successful, white, unless used as a highlight, requires its own space, possibly within some secret and enclosed area where its impact will be absolute and complete. For this a background of formally arranged, clipped yew is ideal. Where this is not a possibility, then a boundary clothed in some dark evergreen, such as ivy, would suffice as well. Within this enclosure light plays an important role. Overhead daylight with the presence of a strong summer sun will do little for the colours beyond reducing them to a uniform drabness. To excel, they must enjoy the benefit of shade.

Probably one of the most famous of all white gardens, this one at Sissinghurst Castle in Kent was created by Vita Sackville-West in the years immediately following the Second World War.

Helleborus niger The Christmas rose brings cheer to the garden in the early part of the year. Plant in a slightly shaded situation. E, ○, 45 × 45cm/1.5 × 1.5ft

***Narcissus* 'Flower Drift'** Many of the white flowered daffodils would be most suitable for a pale scheme. 45 × 45cm/ 1.5 × 1.5ft

***Camellia japonica* 'Nobilissima'** The pure white flowerhead of this early camellia is particularly enticing. E, 3 × 2m/10 × 6ft

Syringa vulgaris A white form of the common lilac for spring colour. A hardy shrub. 6 × 4m/20 × 13ft

Erythronium californicum **'White Beauty'** Erythroniums are especially attractive spring bulbs for a lightly shaded area. ◑, 30 × 20cm/1ft × 8in

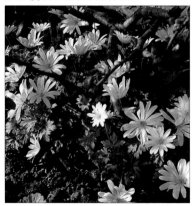

Tulipa **'Purissima'** Spring-flowering bulbs are a must in any garden. 40 × 20cm/16 × 8in

Anemone blanda **'White Splendour'** Scatter these tiny bulbs beneath shrubs to enjoy flowers in the spring. 10cm/4in

Prunus 'Tai Haku' The Great White Cherry is spectacular in flower. 8 × 8m/ 26 × 26ft

Viburnum plicatum 'Mariesii' Flat white flower corymbs in the late spring and first part of the summer. 3 × 4m/10 × 13ft

Geranium macrorrhizum 'Album' A spreading, hardy perennial to use as ground cover under and around trees and shrubs. 60 × 60cm/2 × 2ft

Tiarella cordifolia Feathery white racemes appear from the late spring well into early summer. 30 × 30cm/1 × 1ft

Libertia formosa Flowers throughout spring. A hardy perennial. Semi-E, 1 × 1m/3 × 3ft

***Wisteria floribunda* 'Alba'** Wisteria is grown for its long flower racemes in early summer. ○, 9m/30ft

***Cistus* 'Paladin'** A shrub for a hot, dry, sunny site. Paper-white flower petals are blotched a deep wine red and are carried over glossy, dark green leaves. ○, E, 2 × 2m/6 × 6ft

Centranthus ruber albus Perennial valerian is likely to seed around. Continuous colour from early summer. 1m × 45cm/ 3 × 1.5ft

Sidalcea candida A flowering period from early summer until autumn from this herbaceous perennial. 1m × 75cm/ 3 × 2.5ft

A lovely grouping of perennials. Note how seedlings are permitted, adding to the relaxed atmosphere. Included are *Lychnis coronaria* 'Alba', astrantia and poppies.

Iris orientalis A perennial iris flowering in the late spring and early summer. 60 × 60cm/2 × 2ft

Nicotiana The fragrant tobacco plant is most usually grown as an annual. Plant in sun. 30 × 15cm/1ft × 6in

***Rosa* 'Iceberg'** Early summer is the time for roses. Of all the floribunda roses 'Iceberg' retains its popularity. These blooms, which appear for an extended season, sustain colour in an all white garden. 1.2 × 1.2m/4 × 4ft

Lilium regale Summer-flowering lilies, deeply scented, are one of the joys of the garden. This one is no exception. Seen here, it is planted in a border where, given good drainage, the bulbs will flower for many years. 1.2m/4ft

***Lilium* 'Olivia'** Bulbous lilies may be successfully grown in pots. 1.2m/4ft

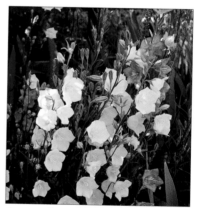

Campanula latiloba alba Summer-flowering, this is a perennial for any white garden. 1.2m × 30cm/4 × 1ft

Campanula persicifolia The white form of this perennial, in midsummer, is emphasized by the blue. ○, 1m × 30cm/ 3 × 1ft

***Clematis viticella* 'Little Nell'** This late summer viticella is white with pink. 3–3.6m/10–12ft

Leucanthemum* × *superbum Shasta daisies are tough perennials with which to fill late summer borders. 1.2 × 1m/4 × 3ft

Malva moschata alba An easy perennial which will spread in most normal garden soils. 60 × 60cm/2 × 2ft

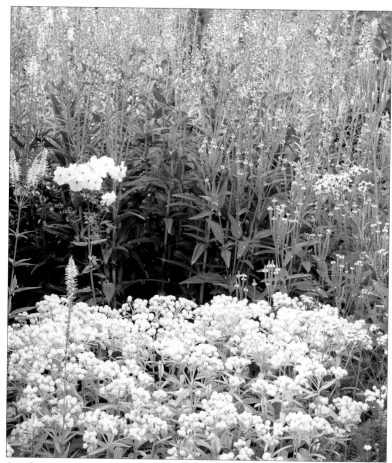

An ethereal quality is achieved in a large border. Tall spires of *Veronicastrum virginicum* provide a backdrop to the paper-like flowers of *Anaphalis margaritacea*.

Anemone* × *hybrida Japanese anemones must be amongst the most accommodating of all garden plants. Perennial and hardy, they cover the ground and flower for weeks from late summer onwards. 1.5m × 60cm/5 × 2ft

***Echinacea purpurea* 'White Swan'** One of the most admired of all late summer perennials on account of its green tinted petals and centre. Cone flowers will thrive in most garden soils. 1.2m × 75cm/4 × 2.5ft

***Artemisia lactiflora* Guizhou Group**
Airy flowers on this perennial which is
suited to the front of the border as to the
rear. 1m × 60cm/3 × 2ft

Cosmos Include annual white cosmos in
summer bedding schemes. Prefers sun.
60cm/2ft

***Crinum × powellii* 'Album'** Bulbs of late summer crinums prefer to be planted in a
sheltered position, possibly against a wall and to be given free draining soil.
◑, 1m × 60cm/3 × 2ft

Magnolia grandiflora This slow growing variety blooms at the end of summer. Best in shelter. ○, E, 10 × 10m/33 × 33ft

Dahlia Dahlias are not frost hardy. Most flower at the year's end. From 30cm/1ft

Gladiolus These flowers for summer come from corms which must be lifted at the first frosts. ○, 1.2m × 30cm/4 × 1ft

Cimicifuga simplex A late flowering perennial producing spikes well into autumn. 1m × 60cm/3 × 2ft

Colchicum autumnale **'Album'** These are autumn-flowering bulbs to naturalize in grass. 20 × 20cm/8 × 8in

CONSIDER ALSO:

SHRUBS:
Carpenteria
  californica
  (summer)
Magnolia stellata
  'Royal Star'
  (spring)
Romneya coulteri
  (sum–aut)
ANNUALS:
Argemone
  grandiflora

PERENNIALS:
Astilbe
  'Deutschland'
  (summer)
Pulmonaria
  officinalis
  'Sissinghurst
  White' (spring)
BULBS:
Crocus chrysanthus
  'Snow Bunting'
  (early spring)

Cyclamen hederifolium **f.** *album* These little bulbs are autumn-flowering. Leaves are attractive. Following immediately after the flowers, they are ivy-shaped of silvery green. 10 × 20cm/4 × 8in

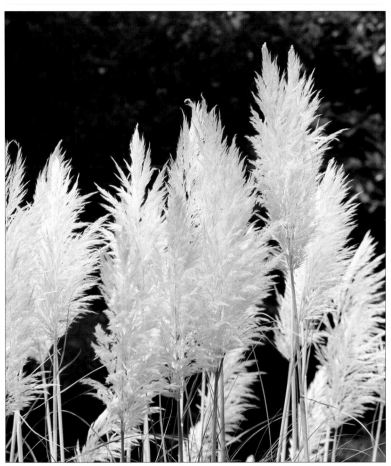

Cortaderia selloana The pampas grass at the end of the year. Cut back hard to the ground each spring but wear gloves as the leaves are sharp. 2 × 1.2m/6 × 4ft

Grey

First and foremost, grey is invaluable for separating colours which do not combine well together and which result in the most horrible of clashes.

Second, rather in the manner of white, grey helps to shape a border, to give it visual balance and form.

But, more than anything else, grey is such a wonderful partner to other plants. For a really moody, even gothic, effect, then combine it with deep purple or darkest magenta. Where a soft, dreamy picture is appropriate, then place it among pinks, lemons, lavenders and greens. For something much more startling and daring, mix grey with the lacquer red of a Chinese bridge or position it with the brown of a Russian bear. And, most difficult of all, use grey with black. The results are stunning!

Here grey is seen at its most architectural. The onopordum is deliberately chosen to tower over the alliums to give a sense of drama to this border which has been formally edged with box.

Ghost-grey leaves of the curry plant, *Helichrysum italicum*, appear to float over the grey-green rue, *Ruta graveolens*.

Stachys byzantina has been imaginatively used here to highlight the purple foliage of *Lysimachia ciliata* 'Firecracker'.

Grey shrubs and perennials help to create depth and space in a border. Placed with care they may also either highlight other plantings or, indeed, tone down those which may approach the garish.

151

Blue and grey successfully combine together, as illustrated here, to make for a cool interlude within a planting scheme. Not only do the mid-blues look well with grey, but also those which are darker.

Verbascum olympicum Mulleins are surely amongst the loveliest of perennials. 2m × 60cm/6 × 2ft

Scotch thistles have been positioned with the spike-forming fox-tail lily, *Eremurus stenophyllus* ssp. *stenophyllus*.

Through the deep, plum-coloured leaves of the *Heuchera micrantha* 'Palace Purple' the finely cut foliage of the silvery *Artemisia* 'Powis Castle' appears to weave a magical spell.

This anaphalis, shown in the foreground, brings a certain unity to the other colours in the border.

Fine grey foliage, such as is to be found on this tanacetum, is best when seen in contrast.

153

At the base of the burgundy cotinus a broad band of silver-leafed artemisia strikes a forceful contrast. The cotinus may be hard pruned each spring to promote new, richly coloured growth.

Scale in the garden is important. A low wall of the compact shrub, *Berberis thunbergii* 'Bagatelle', is shown off by the non-flowering, *Stachys byzantina* 'Silver Carpet'.

Tall growing stachys amongst other varied colours. In this way the eye is given rest.

Cineraria, with grey leaves, has been included, like a mark of punctuation in a sentence.

The cool, yet dramatic effect of grey *Artemisia ludoviciana* 'Valerie Finnis', white achillea and a note of acid green introduced in the foliage of *Achillea grandifolia*.

Eryngium* × *zabelii Crowding the front of the border are these summer-flowering perennial plants with their flower heads, ideal for the flower arranger either fresh or dried. ◑, 45 × 25cm/1.5ft × 10in

Silver-grey artemisia acts as a screen, turning yellow anthemis gold.

Tanacetum haradjanii This tansy is grown for foliage. Contrast it with any dark flower. ◑, 60 × 60cm/2 × 2ft

Here anaphalis is a backdrop to summer-flowering border phlox. All greys associate well with pink to mauve and may be used as underplanting and ground cover.

Brachyglottis (Senecio) 'Sunshine' This shrub in summer is covered in yellow flowers. ◐, E, 1 × 1.5m/3 × 5ft

CONSIDER ALSO:	
SHRUBS AND	*Eucalyptus gunnii*
TREES:	*Pyrus salicifolia*
Ballota	'Pendula'

Black

Black as a colour within the garden must, inevitably, be limited to flowers of the darkest hue, to foliage of a similar nature and to the stems of many shrubs and trees, most apparent in wintertime. A really black grass, however, does exist, *Ophiopogon planiscapus* 'Nigrescens', sometimes known as Black Dragon, which is most effective in a mass.

The impact of black in the garden must lie in the way in which it is combined with other plants to create a sense of mystery, or to be used for dramatic effect.

Tulipa **'Queen of Night'** looks striking against silver-grey *Cynara cardunculus*. 45cm/1.5ft

Tulipa **'Black Parrot'** Plant in large groups for best results as tulips, and these are no exception, are so much better in a mass. Try them too in containers to be taken indoors at flowering time. 45cm/1.5ft

***Aquilegia vulgaris* 'Magpie'** Columbines remain a perennial favourite for the early summer border. Plant with dark purples. 1m × 45cm/3 × 1.5ft

***Viola* 'Bowles' Black'** Grown at the base of a yew hedge they will reinforce a sombre look. 10 × 30cm/4in × 1ft

Helleborus orientalis Hellebores with their evergreen foliage, are wonderful perennial plants for the spring. ◑, E, 45 × 45cm/1.5 × 1.5ft

***Ophiopogon planiscapus* 'Nigrescens'** This perennial grass is able to look effective with so many other plants. 25 × 25cm/10 × 10in

Colour Combinations

The colour of one flower affects our perception of the colour of the flower next to it. Some of the most successful colour combinations are shown on the following pages.

Yellow with White

Soft, pale yellows are the colours of springtime and early summer. Not for now the strong golds of late summer and autumn, but gentle tints which suggest rather than state. Teamed with white they take on a lightness of tone.

Such a combination is seldom commonplace. It remains both subtle and suggestive, an understatement, demanding of close observation. Enjoy them particularly in the evening as the light fades when they will take on a luminosity which is, at times, unforgettable.

Spires of verbascum glow in this summer scheme. Intermingling are feverfew, *Tanacetum parthenium*.

Rosa 'Canary Bird' and *Veronica gentianoides* 'Tissington White' are the principal players in this yellow and white spring border. Creamy *Aquilegia* 'Edelweiss' provides a link between the two.

Wonderfully warm, butter-yellow heads of *Tulipa* 'Maréchal Niel' crown a carpet of white Universal pansies in this highly imaginative and very successful scheme.

Open blooms of *Rosa rugosa* 'Alba' with the yellow and white feverfew (*Tanacetum parthenium*).

Foxgloves over yellow Jerusalem sage (*Phlomis fruticosa*), with an early summer rose.

Colour has been carefully managed in this garden. Yellow, white, and of course green, have been gathered together to create an informal planting area which remains restful.

Lilium 'Golden Splendor', adding a touch of the exotic to a white and yellow border. Lilies prefer full sun and free draining soil. Because of this they are often grown in pots.

White honesty, *Lunaria annua alba*, a biennial, with tulips in this display for spring.

White lilies stand out against the ice-blue eryngiums in this border.

Yellow with Red

Employ these strong colours together
to create schemes which are hot, fiery
and exciting. These are not shades to
mix for those who like their gardens
to be restful and easy on the eye. These
are the colours to startle and surprise.

Setting is always important. A plain,
dark background will set off these
colours and avoid confusion where
they mingle with paler shades.

This is a combination which is easy
to achieve later in the year when the
strong reds and yellows of heleniums
mix with yellow rudbeckias and red
echinaceas.

Lime-yellow bracts of *Euphorbia
polychroma* with the dusky-red flowers of
Geum rivale in early summer.

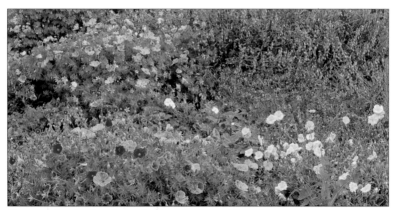

Orange, red and yellow helianthemums (rock roses) in early summer create a tapestry.
The pinky-mauve cranesbills lead the eye away from the hot tones.

Mahogany-red *Helenium* 'Moerheim Beauty' is toned down by creamy-yellow *Aconitum lycoctonum* ssp. *vulparia*.

Lobelia 'Compliment Scarlet', over *Santolina chamaecyparissus* 'Lemon Queen' in a contrast of colour and form.

With its soft, velvety foliage and creamy flowers *Verbascum nigrum* is the ideal companion to this blood-red, late summer helenium for end of season excitement.

Yellow with Blue and Purple

Yellow with blue is a classic combination. Put with purple it is more unusual. The first is suggestive of the early part of the year. The second comes into its own as summer gathers pace. Yellow is a colour to which the eye is automatically drawn. Linking it with another colour, such as blue, reduces its force and, if lemon is used, brings it into the pastel range. With purple, gold and deep tones give a stronger impression, a heaviness even, which may require a lift with white, grey or silver.

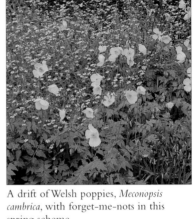

A drift of Welsh poppies, *Meconopsis cambrica*, with forget-me-nots in this spring scheme.

Both these blue irises and yellow mimulus enjoy the moist soil on this bankside.

Yellow hemerocallis (day lilies) with china-blue cranesbill.

Buttermilk anthemis are complemented by scabious and phygelius.

Delphiniums are grown here with the pompon flowers of *Gentiana lutea*.

Pale mauve *Campanula lactiflora* is teamed with the homely yellow of *Verbascum nigrum*.

Scabious flowers contrast here with the flat heads of achillea.

In spring the Welsh poppy, *Meconopsis cambrica*, intermingles with bluebells, *Hyacinthoides non-scriptus*.

In this spring border the brightest yellow are the leaves of *Valeriana phu* 'Aurea'.

Borders like this one in spring have been planned with confidence. Colour is restricted to blue and yellow, and plants are packed together for the greatest possible impact.

Violet-blue is accompanied by citrus yellow. Flowers in the foreground are *Asphodeline lutea*.

Coreopsis verticillata against which is grown the thistle heads of *Eryngium × zabelii*. Both plants are perennial and hardy.

Bold clumps of *Anthemis tinctoria* 'E.C. Buxton' are placed at regular intervals, whilst nepetas, salvias, and helianthus, yet to flower, are included not simply for colour but for texture and form.

Blue with White

Together these colours make for cool schemes. This is a combination to follow an area of the garden which is devoted to warm shades. Most often the same flower is to be found in both blue and white, and effective schemes may be devised by using drifts of each in the same border. However, caution should be exercised in the positioning. Blue, unlike white, recedes and it is easy to finish up with an arrangement which is lacking in definition.

Rounded heads of border phlox are sharpened by the intense blue of the hardy agapanthus.

These white love-in-a-mist (*Nigella*) surround the palest of blue flowers of the *Polemonium* (Jacob's ladder).

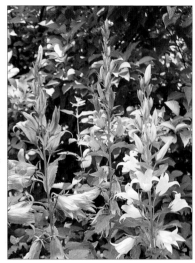

The effect of mixing the same plant in different colours: blue and white *Campanula latifolia*.

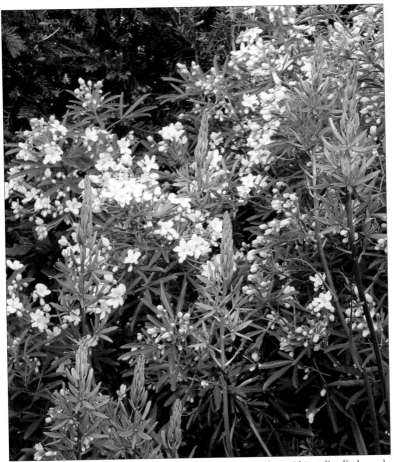

Sweetly scented flowers of the Mexican orange blossom, *Choisya* 'Aztec Pearl', through which rise tall spires of blue camassia, *Camassia leichtlinii*, so that they become an integral part of the shrub.

White flowers of *Clematis montana* with mauve-blue *Abutilon* × *suntense* in the late spring.

Growing to 10 × 7.5cm/4 × 3in, *Anemone appenina* will produce flowers in springtime.

In the late spring. *Clematis montana* among the flowers of *Ceanothus* 'Blue Mound'. This clematis type is exceedingly vigorous and it is likely to choke the host shrub.

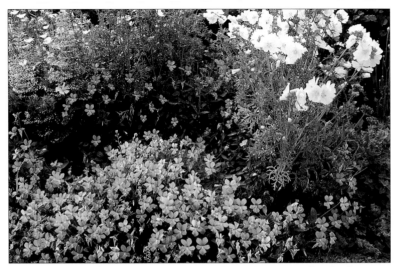

Although not strictly blue, the flowers of the violet, *Viola cornuta*, make a lovely contrast with the taller growing, white flowers of *Malva moschata alba*.

Ice-white bells of *Campanula persicifolia* are placed here with the yellow flowers of a perennial potentilla.

Eryngiums with white eschscholtzia, an annual which will flower summer to autumn.

175

Lavender with Pinks and Reds

Misty lavender-blues combine with quiet pinks and rich reds to produce borders of pensive beauty through summer months. They are a foil to harsh sunlight and glare. Such blues are non-assertive, lacking the intensity of a clear blue, conveying a sense of distance. They blend with muted pinks and reds to resemble slightly faded damasks. These colours are the familiar mainstay of the garden, in possession of an unassuming elegance.

Universal pansies, 'True Blue', are placed amongst random drifts of the colourful daisy, *Bellis* 'Medicis', to create an arresting yet utterly pleasing combination.

Here the violet-blue flowers of *Campanula lactiflora* tone with the Gallica rose, *Rosa* 'Président de Sèze'.

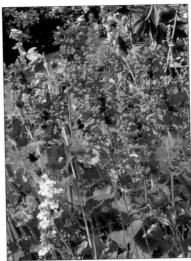

Purple flowers of *Stachys macrantha* 'Robusta' harmonize with *Campanula lactiflora* 'Telham Beauty'.

Violet-crimson flowers of the rambling *Rosa* 'Bleu Magenta' pick up the veining of the geranium.

Rosa gallica officinalis, the red rose of Lancaster, plays host to *Clematis integrifolia*.

Velvet-red *Clematis viticella* 'Madame Julia Correvon' with *Clematis viticella* 'Venosa Violacea' in late summer.

The magenta *Lychnis coronaria* against the purple of a summer-flowering buddleja.

A composition for the early summer of plantings of pale pink roses and hardy geraniums. Plant varieties have been deliberately kept to a few, and all within a colour range.

Violas and lamium in pink, mauve and lavender at the front of an herbaceous border.

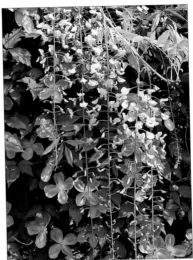

Clematis montana 'Tetrarose' climbs through the long racemes of *Wisteria floribunda* during late spring.

Deep claret orach, *Atriplex hortensis* var. *rubra*, is a foil in this setting to the pale pink cranesbill.

A *Geranium cinereum* 'Ballerina', a lavender and white viola and summer-flowering diascias.

179

Massed Colour

Massed schemes, perhaps because they bring to mind municipal parks and gardens, are somehow associated with bright, occasionally vulgar, effects. This need not be the case, and quieter plantings should not be overlooked. When massing any kind of colour, be bold and decisive. Skimping on plants will result in an arrangement that looks thin, half-hearted and lacking in confidence. Too many colours will suggest uncertainty and will be in danger of losing direction. Remember, it is most often the simplest of ideas that work the best.

Bulbs are, of course, a particularly good way to achieve a massed display. Where change is required, then they may be interplanted with something different at the start of each new season.

Ribbons of colour make for a different way of displaying spring favourites. Here the main components are *Tulipa* 'Golden Melody', wallflowers, 'Scarlet Bedding' and Universal pansies.

Bulbs have been set in such a way as to thrust their way through other spring bedding. Here buttery-yellow wallflowers, which must be set out in the previous autumn, contrast with the tulip flowers.

A simple use of tulips which are allowed to drift through this border. The underplanting of forget-me-nots lifts the deep colour of the bulbs and gives to the whole scheme a lightness and airiness.

This somewhat eclectic mix of rock roses, cranesbill and pansies are, in fact, in harmony.

Old-fashioned favourites, such as pansies and the hardy geraniums give a feeling of a cottage garden.

Had these geraniums and helianthemums been planted singly, then little impression would have been made. As it is, planted in the company of others, the overall effect is of one body of colour.

Spires of *Verbena bonariensis* soar over deep pink *Salvia viridis*.

Annual marguerites and fuchsias make a display which should be long lasting.

Roses and peonies, two of the most splendid of all garden plants, convey a sense of luxury to any border. Together they give a wonderfully rich display in early summer.

Colour in the Border

Borders without colour would, it has to be admitted, be rather dull. After all, one of the principal delights of gardening has to be the arrangement of harmonious living pictures which will give satisfaction and be pleasing to the eye for as long a period as possible. That said, the organization of colour is not straightforward. Plants, as we all know only too well, are fickle. Invariably they fail to grow exactly as expected, or, most likely, prove reluctant to flower at the very moment that is absolutely essential to the whole border composition.

Such pitfalls are not easily overcome and much will depend on trial and error, learning to work with your conditions, knowing your plants, resolving mistakes and building on successes.

Limiting the colour range is often one way of bringing about a pleasing result. That is not to say your borders have to be of a single colour. Rather, select plants which will flower within a controlled range, perhaps employing a variety of shades and tints which are based on two or three main colours.

Rose, pink, magenta, a touch of violet, bronze, these colours, all within the same range, contribute a sense of unity to this mainly herbaceous border.

A huge yew buttress makes a splendid background to this border which comprises perennials.

Purple-leafed foliage at either end of the border serves to create balance.

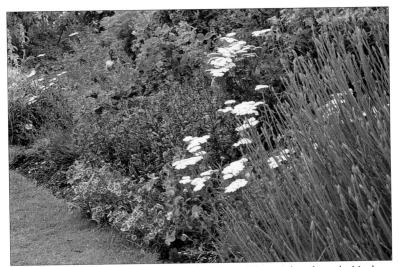

White achillea is used here to punctuate this border of deep pink and purple. Much thought has been given to the grouping to produce a gently undulating effect.

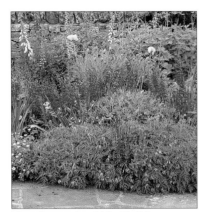

Note the way in which *Gladiolus communis byzantinus* has been placed as a ribbon of colour.

Excellent use of soft yellow, found in the lupins and irises, and white.

Plants in profusion in complementary colours are the mark of this border seen at the start of summer.

Midsummer, and this border is seen at its best. Purple headed alliums, heleniums, phlox and coreopsis are all planted in generous clumps to give a furnished look.

Late summer lavender-mauve, deep pink and purple using asters, cone flowers (*Echinacea purpurea*) and *Verbena bonariensis*.

Autumn Colours

The dying days of the gardening
year produce some of its richest
colouring. With certain plants this is
their greatest season, but there are
also many which reward with a final
display after earning their keep in
spring and summer.

Autumn Foliage

Autumn colour on a grand scale is difficult to achieve in a garden setting and, never more so, where space is restricted. But this does not mean that spectacular effects cannot be achieved. By choosing trees and shrubs with care, and selecting those which will perform well in other seasons too, it is perfectly possible to bring to the smallest of gardens much of the drama which is so typical of this time of year. Among those to consider are birches, cherries, maples, rowans, sumachs and whitebeams as well as colourful dogwoods and the spindle berries.

What of course cannot be ignored is the difficulty of managing late colour in the garden. As the year progresses, and the autumn hues gather force, so summer colour is becoming fast spent and it is too often against a background of dead and decaying perennials that these flashes of brilliance and glory are to be enjoyed. Try, therefore, to position your end-of-season display in such a way as it may be viewed without other distractions. If this is not totally possible, then a little timely cutting back and clearing will help matters considerably.

Pseudolarix amabilis For beauty and hardiness, and where space is not a problem, grow the golden larch. As autumn approaches so leaves turn yellow. 18 × 18m/52 × 52ft

Betula pendula Silver birch is suitable for sunny or shady conditions. Spring catkins and yellow autumn foliage make this a tree for all seasons. 10 × 7.5m/33 × 25ft

Acer campestre Easy and hardy, this acer is best reserved for the wild garden. In a more restricted area, select one of many smaller growing varieties offered by nurseries. 10 × 8m/33 × 26ft

Larix decidua The common larch is a vigorous, deciduous tree, suitable for most soils except very wet or dry, shallow chalk. Larch is a woodland tree making it inappropriate for a normal garden. 20 × 15m/66 × 49ft

Sorbus alnifolia Heavily veined burnt copper leaves at the close of the season. 10 × 10m/33 × 33ft

Nyssa sylvatica The Tupelo has spectacular autumn foliage. For sun, moist soil. 16 × 12m/52 × 39ft

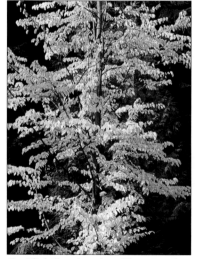

Cercidiphyllum japonicum The seasonal display compensates for insignificant flowers earlier on. 15 × 12m/49 × 39ft

***Acer japonicum* 'Vitifolium'** This shrub, a Japanese maple, has fan-shaped leaves. 4.5 × 4.5m/15 × 15ft

Acer obtusatum A maple whose leaves turn a fiery red in the later part of the year. 15 × 5m/49 × 16ft

Liquidamber styraciflua Unsuitable for shallow chalk, liquidamber prefers moist, well drained soil. 16 × 8m/52 × 26ft

Acer palmatum atropurpureum One of the most beautiful of maples. Finely cut leaves and graceful arching stems never appear out of place. 4.5 × 4.5m/15 × 15ft

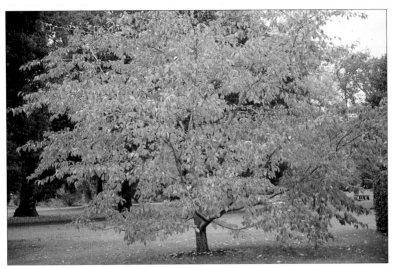

***Prunus* × *yedoensis* 'Yoshino'** The spreading branches of the Yoshino Cherry carry white flowers in the early spring to be followed by bronze-orange foliage at the year's end. 8 × 8m/26 × 26ft

***Acer palmatum* 'Senkaki'** The Coral Bark Maple has coral-red branches, effective in winter. 4.5 × 4.5m/15 × 15ft

Acer palmatum Japanese maples have outstanding autumn colour. 4.5 × 4.5m/ 15 × 15ft

Sorbus sargentiana Of rigidly branched habit, this rowan with red leaf stalks colours vividly in autumn, topped by large rounded heads of small scarlet fruits. 8 × 8m/ 26 × 26ft

Enkianthus perulatus White flowers in spring, but it is the autumn colour which makes this such a desirable plant. Must be grown on neutral or acidic soil. 3 × 3m/ 10 × 10ft

Disanthus cercidifolius Few shrubs can rival this excellent specimen for its range of autumn colours. An acid lover, this shrub should be planted in free-draining soil. 3 × 3m/10 × 10ft

***Viburnum plicatum* 'Mariesii'** This shrub requires sufficient space to show itself off. Huge white flowers produce an abundant spring display. Easy. 3 × 3m/10 × 10ft

Euonymus alatus Dull, bronzy-green leaves turn to flame on this slow shrub. 3 × 3m/10 × 10ft

Viburnum recognitum This variety has yellow foliage at turn of year. 3 × 3m/10 × 10ft

Rhus typhina The staghorn sumach is renowned for its shape as well as its colour at the close of the year. Erect seed heads continue through the winter. 5 × 6m/16 × 20ft

Fothergilla major Fragrant white flowers in spring and autumn colour. Slow growing, best planted in moist, acidic soil. 3 × 3m/10 × 10ft

***Cercis canadensis* 'Forest Pansy'** A slow growing form. 10 × 10m/33 × 33ft

***Roga rugosa* 'Alba'** In autumn they carry scarlet heps. 1.5 × 1.5m/5 × 5ft

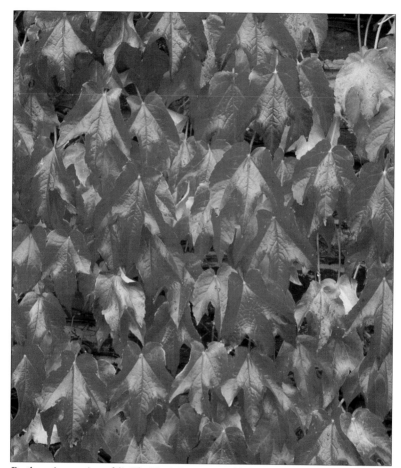

Parthenocissus quinquefolia The Virginia creeper, self-clinging, is capable of covering an entire house with its deeply cut leaves which redden as the year advances. 12m/39ft

Cotoneaster horizontalis Throughout the period small red berries add decoration, unless raided by birds. It is possible to train this particular form against a wall.
2 × 2m/6 × 6ft

CONSIDER ALSO:

TREES:
*Crataegus ×
    prunifolia*

SHRUBS:
Cotinus coggygria
    'Royal Purple'

CLIMBERS:
*Parthenocissus
    henryana*
Vitis coignetiae
Vitis vinifera
    'Brandt'

***Berberis thunbergii* 'Atropurpurea'**
Decked with long-lasting scarlet berries.
2 × 2m/6 × 6ft

Fruits and Berries

Showy fruits and berries are, in the main, one of the delights of autumn. Appearing at the same time as brilliantly coloured leaves, they add an additional sparkle and interest to trees and shrubs in the closing days of the year. But whereas fading foliage, however magnificent, is representative of decay and, of course, death, seasonal fruits are the culmination of nature's cycle and are a symbol of ripeness and richness.

Clinging on, as they so often do, into the depths of winter, until ravaged by hungry birds, fruits and berries take on a new lease of life when masked in hoar frost or lightly dusted with a coating of fresh snow. Then they become an exciting and integral part of a winter landscape which, in its own way, is as varied and interesting as that which is enjoyed during the long days of summer.

Cotoneaster frigidus **'Cornubia'** This hybrid is noted for its scarlet berries. Where cream and yellow fruits are preferred, then grow the form *Cotoneaster frigidus* 'Fructu Luteo'. 7 × 7m/23 × 23ft

***Viburnum opulus* 'Xanthocarpum'**
Early autumn berries ripen on this shrub.
4.5 × 4.5m/15 × 15ft

***Malus × zumi* 'Golden Hornet'** From
late summer well into winter golden crabs
crowd this small tree. 4 × 6m/13 × 20ft

***Sorbus* 'Joseph Rock'** Mountain ashes
are easily accommodated in gardens.
12 × 7m/39 × 23ft

***Cotoneaster salicifolius* 'Exburyensis'** An
excellent, evergreen shrub which is well
worth seeking out. 5 × 5m/16 × 16ft

Sorbus vilmorinii After the flowers these pale pink berries appear. 5 × 5m/ 16 × 16ft

***Sorbus cashmiriana* 'Rosiness'** A small tree which may be grown as a shrub. 5 × 5m/16 × 16ft

Sorbus sargentiana These berries of late summer, provide rich colour. 5 × 5m/ 16 × 16ft

***Sorbus* 'Winter Cheer'** The berries of this mountain ash will last. 12 × 7m/39 × 23ft

***Malus* × *robusta* 'Red Sentinel'** As the leaves of this small crab fall, so these apples are revealed which are ignored by birds at least until the worst of winter. 4 × 6m/ 13 × 20ft

Viburnum betulifolium White flowers of summer, scarlet berries of autumn. 4.5 × 4.5m/15 × 15ft

Viburnum opulus The guelder rose. White flowers early summer, then berries. 4.5 × 4.5m/15 × 15ft

Rosa moyesii **'Geranium'** Blood-red flowers of the early summer are followed later on with these heps which decorate the stems throughout autumn. 2.4 × 2.2m/8 × 7ft

Cornus kousa The Chinese dogwood is a
shrub with white flowers in summer.
3.6 × 4m/12 × 13ft

Berberis thunbergii As autumn approaches
stems are lined with red berries.
1.2 × 1.2m/4 × 4ft

Of all berrying shrubs, pyracanthas are amongst the most distinctive. Wall-trained, they
bring life to shady sides of a house.

207

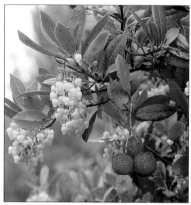

Arbutus unedo The Killarney strawberry tree will tolerate some lime. E, 5 × 5m/ 16 × 16ft

Photinia davidiana A shrub which bears bunches of berries. E, 6 × 4m/20 × 13ft

Hypericum × inodorum 'Elstead' These plants are prone to rust in most gardens. 1.2 × 1.2m/4 × 4ft

Euonymus europaeus Perfectly happy on chalk, the spindle tree is alight in autumn. A named variety to look out for is *Euonymus europaeus* 'Red Cascade'. 4.5 × 4.5m/ 15 × 15ft

Euonymus cornutus* var. *quinquecornutus Evergreen in mild areas, this shrub is adorned in autumn with extraordinary berries. 2 × 2m/6 × 6ft

Callicarpa bodinieri* var. *geraldii This shrub turns purple and produces remarkable berries. 4 × 4m/13 × 13ft

Pernettya (Gaultheria) mucronata Shrub will produce berries of white, pink, red, purple or black. Acid soil.
◯, E, 75cm × 1.2m/2.5 × 4ft

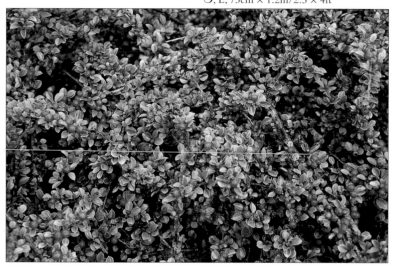

Of all garden shrubs, cotoneasters are hardy, quick-growing and easy in cultivation thriving on most fertile soils providing that they are fairly free draining.

***Arum italicum* 'Pictum'** As the marbled leaves of this perennial disappear, it berries. ●, 25 × 20cm/10 × 8in

Iris foetidissima Seed pods of the Gladwin iris burst open in winter. E, 45 × 60cm/1.5 × 2ft

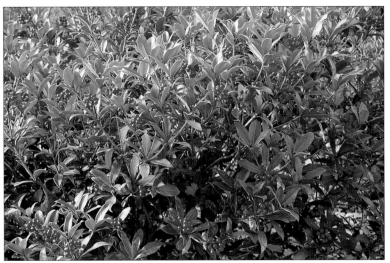

Skimmia japonica To effect pollination of skimmias, plant male and female varieties together. There is a so-called hermaphrodite cultivar, *Skimmia japonica* 'Veitchii'. All will succeed in partial or complete shade.

Bark and Stems

At their most striking in wintertime, trees, free of the distraction of leaf cover, make an exciting contribution to the garden scene.

At this period it is, of course, the colour of bark which is likely to be noticed. But also its richness of colour, pattern and textural quality which is particularly welcome out of season.

Acer griseum The paperbark maple. Autumn leaves are red and gold. 8 × 6m/ 26 × 20ft

Eucalyptus pauciflora **ssp.** *niphophila* Plant in a position out of reach of cold winds. ○, E, 10 × 8m/33 × 26ft

Cornus alba Grow this easy shrub for its stems which light up a winter border. 3 × 3m/10 × 10ft

***Salix alba vitellina* 'Britzensis'** Treat this shrubby willow to the same hard pruning as for Cornus alba. 3 × 3m/10 × 10ft

***Cornus stolonifera* 'Flaviramea'** All winter the stems of this dogwood contribute colour. In summer small white flowers are produced, but these lack any significance. 2 × 4m/6 × 12ft

Stuartia sinensis Plant in a lightly shaded spot in moist soil rich in humus.
4.5 × 4.5m/15 × 15ft

Acer capillipes One of the snake bark maples noted for the white stripes down the bark. 10 × 8m/33 × 26ft

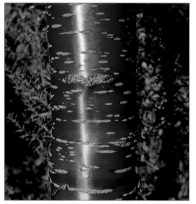

Prunus serrula Rich mahogany bark of this cherry polished by winter sunshine.
9 × 9m/30 × 30ft

Betula ermanii This is a tree for the border or as a lawn specimen. 15 × 4.5m/ 49 × 15ft

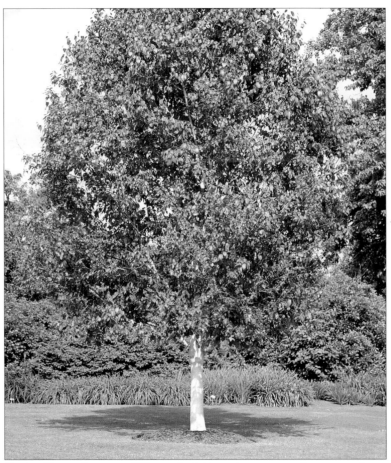

Betula utilis* var. *jacquemontii The trunk of this specimen tree stands out even when cloaked in leaves. In autumn foliage turns golden. 15 × 5m/49 × 16ft

Colour Around the Garden

Colour need not be restricted to beds and borders and their grand set-piece displays when warmer days arrive. There are many ways for a gardener to bring colour to other areas.

Alpine and Rock Garden

Most alpine and rock plants require good drainage. They much prefer to be planted in a gritty medium through which water will readily run. For many, the worst of the winter weather is nothing to being water-logged or to having water, even ice, collecting around the crown. Many, but by no means all, enjoy the warmth of the sun, something to bear in mind when establishing a new rock garden.

A visit to an alpine nursery will give a good indication of just how many rock plants there are. Choose from minute columbines, like the violet-blue *Aquilegia bertolonii*, miniature pinks like *Dianthus* 'Inshriach Dazzler' or *Dianthus* 'La Bourboule', even a miniature cotton lavender, *Santolina elegans*. The list is endless and, ultimately, choice will reflect personal taste.

A colourful mixture of rock plants. In this garden the plan has clearly been to create a tapestry of colour rather than to consider a more limited, restricted scheme. A path allows for inspection of the plants.

Fritillaria pyrenaica From the Pyrenees, and known as the Pyrenean snakeshead, this bulb produces these lovely flower heads of dusky purple, chequered with yellow, in the spring of each year. 30cm/1ft

Pulsatilla vulgaris rubra Flowering at Easter, this is a long-lived perennial. 30 × 30cm/1 × 1ft

Pulsatilla vulgaris Normally deep purple, this form is of a pale lilac. 30 × 30cm/ 1 × 1ft

Sempervivums, or house leeks, make splendid subjects with which to fill containers.

Erinus alpinus A short lived perennial. Pink flowers in early summer. ○, E, 2.5–5cm/1–2in

***Ajuga reptans* 'Pink Surprise'** A form of bugle. Foliage is evergreen. 15 × 60cm/ 6in × 2ft

Purple aubrieta and yellow alyssum. Cut back hard once the flowering is over.

Dianthus **'Gravetye Gem'** Old-fashioned pinks are one of the delights of the garden in summer not only for their pretty flowers but also for their heavenly scent.
○, E, 15 × 30cm/6in × 1ft

Lamium maculatum **'Wootton Pink'** A dead nettle which is not invasive. Flowers in summer. 15 × 30cm/6in × 1ft

Diascia cordata Flowers of this small perennial are produced throughout the summer. 20 × 20cm/8 × 8in

Herb and Kitchen Garden

All too often the herb and kitchen gardens are considered purely as functional. True, it has to be said, in recent times there has been a revival of interest in creating formally designed herb gardens where the emphasis is firmly placed on pattern, colour and form rather than to serve any serious domestic purpose. In small gardens, where space is at a premium, then herbs are often included for their ornamental value in the mixed border.

The same cannot, sadly, be said of vegetables. In too many cases there is a reluctance to grow these other than for their primary purpose, to be eaten. The imaginative gardener will naturally recognize the merits of many vegetables and will wish to include them, not least for their colour, as part of general border schemes.

Summer flowering roses, which may be picked for the house, are central to this formally designed herb garden where sage, rosemary and chives, for kitchen use, are included.

This French *Lavandula stoechas* is combined here with a pale pink bistort, *Polygonum bistorta*.

This highly ornate corner of a garden demonstrates how a working area can be integrated.

Rows of chard, beetroot and lettuce have been interplanted with nasturtiums.

Yellow evening primrose and lavender with the green leaves of spearmint.

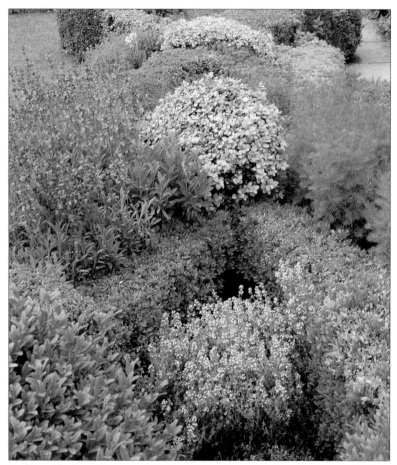

Traditional herb gardens more often than not are based on a formal design in which beds, based on squares and rectangles, are divided by low box hedging.

The onions contained within this box edged bed are arranged to be decorative.

Wavy asparagus foliage provides variation in form and texture to the lettuces.

Runner beans could well be sited at the back of a mixed border.

Colour and form. Here chives and mint jostle with each other for attention.

The Water Garden

You may, if you are very fortunate indeed, be in the enviable position of having natural water, in the form of a stream or a pond, within your garden. Most people, though, have to rely on something which is artificially created and whilst this in itself is not a problem, disguising the installation often is.

It may well be that the best policy is to select plants which will perform well together in a particular season, say spring, and accept that this is the time of year when the water garden will be at its best. For the rest of the year the emphasis will be on maintaining a tidy appearance with, perhaps, the inclusion of a massed, block planting of a single perennial to give flower colour at another time. Planning colour in this way will, except when working on a large scale, give very much more satisfying results.

These candelabra primula make a statement of colour. Contrast is brought about with yellow flag irises and golden sedge, the whole planned for the early summer.

Primula sieboldii This variety of primula flowers in spring in a cool, moist situation.
By midsummer it will have died down. 15 × 15cm/6 × 6in

Primula pulverulenta A form of
candelabra primula in early summer.
60 × 30cm/2 × 1ft

Of all aquatic plants, that is to say those
which grow in water, water lilies remain
favourite.

***Caltha palustris* 'Flore Pleno'** Spring colour with this perennial marsh marigold. 30 × 30cm/1 × 1ft

Primula florindae Bells during summer. Some shade during the day. 75 × 75cm/ 2.5 × 2.5ft

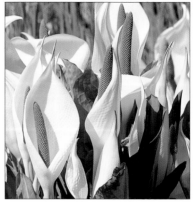

Lysichiton americanus These spathes appear in the spring before leaves develop. 1m × 75cm/3 × 2.5ft

Lysichiton camtschatcensis A white skunk cabbage which is smaller in habit. 75 × 60cm/2.5 × 2ft

Geum rivale **'Leonard's Variety'** The perennial water avens, flowering in spring. 45 × 45cm/1.5 × 1.5ft

Astilbe **'Erica'** All of the summer-flowering astilbes carry these plumes. 1 × 1m/3 × 3ft

Mimulus **'Orange Glow'** This summer perennial is an unusual variety. All mimulus should be planted in moisture retentive soil. 60 × 60cm/2 × 2ft

The Winter Garden

Winter is not, as everyone knows, a season of extravagant colour. And yet it is not without interest. Trees and shrubs, laid bare, reveal their structure and form, vistas, which remain closed in summer, are opened to view.

But it is the flowers in the borders which attract most attention and which give so much pleasure. Here are to be found the earliest of the bulbs – aconites, crocuses and, of course, snowdrops. To these may be added miniature irises and those most wonderful of early flowering perennials, hellebores. Among these, before the *Helleborus orientalis* forms, are those like the Christmas rose (*Helleborus niger*), red stemmed *Helleborus foetidus* 'Wester Flisk' and the beautiful *Helleborus lividus*. Add to this flowering shrubs, coloured conifers, and even a clematis or two, and the picture is very much alive.

Here large evergreen and ruby coloured conifers have been planted with sweeps of winter-flowering heather, *Erica carnea*, in a broad island bed to give a vibrant display of colour.

Iris unguicularis Algerian iris. Ideally, plant in poor soil against a hot, dry wall. E, 20 × 60cm/8in × 2ft

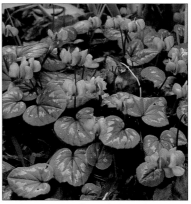

Cyclamen coum Allow hardy cyclamen to colonize underneath deciduous trees. 10cm/4in

***Iris reticulata* 'Harmony'** To increase, propagate by division during late summer. ◑, 10–15cm/4–6in

Galanthus nivalis Position in some shade and divide immediately flowers have gone over. 15 × 15cm/6 × 6in

Eranthis hyemalis Winter aconite flourish in humus-rich soil in semi-shade. 10 × 15cm/4 × 6in

Jasminum nudiflorum This shrub may be trained against a wall or to cover a fence. 3m/10ft

Hamamelis mollis Include this shrub as a centrepiece to the winter border. Witch hazels are slow growing and will take many years before they fill their space. 2.4 × 3m/ 8 × 10ft

Clematis cirrhosa Early evergreen clematis. Afford it shelter. E, 2 × 1m/ 6 × 3ft

Narcissus bulbocodium Planted deeply, these will flower year after year. ○, 15 × 20cm/6 × 8in

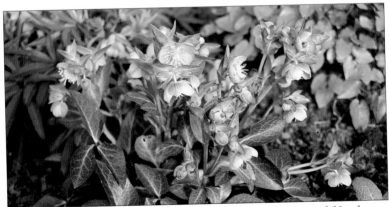

Helleborus lividus The leaves of this hellebore are attractive all year round. Not the hardiest of hellebores so give a sheltered position. E, ◑, 45 × 45cm/1.5 × 1.5ft

Colour in the Conservatory

If you are fortunate enough to own a conservatory, or to have a greenhouse in the garden which you are able to keep free of frost, then you will be able to enjoy year-round colour, even at a time when there is little in flower outside. A visit to a good florist or garden centre should prove to be a most rewarding experience and you will doubtless find yourself spoilt for choice.

But a conservatory does not necessarily have to be entirely for decoration. Any heated space can be utilized as a home for tender perennials which will not overwinter outside or a space in which to keep cuttings of half-hardy favourites.

Do remember that all indoor plants require regular watering and feeding. This is particularly so during the summer months.

Jasminum polyanthum Of immense value in a cool conservatory, this loveliest jasmine will flood fragrance from flowers in late spring. ○, E, 5m/15ft

Anisodontea capensis This sub-shrub will flower all summer and winter too under glass. ◯, 1 × 1m/3 × 3ft

Fuchsia Grow them for their brilliant flower from early summer onwards.

Brugmansia (***Datura***) Angel's trumpets flower during the summer. 1.2 × 1m/ 4 × 3ft

Pelargonium Geraniums are used widely. This is *Pelargonium* 'Madame Layal'.

Thunbergia alata Black-eyed Susan, an easily grown climber in flower for summer. ○, 2m/6ft

Euryops pectinatus A small shrub smothered in daisy flowers. 60 × 60cm/ 2 × 2ft

Clivia miniata Flowers are borne over a long period. In containers this makes a spectacular plant. 60 × 30cm/2 × 1ft

Nerium oleander Best placed outside in summer and returned for winter. 1.2 × 1m/4 × 3ft

Plumbago capensis This climbing shrub flowers in late summer and early autumn. 2m/6ft

***Cymbidium ruspex* 'Ivory Queen'** An orchid which may be grown successfully as a potted plant. 60 × 30cm/2 × 1ft

Pots and Containers

For those with very tiny or even no garden at all, pots are one way of creating colour in a small space. In larger gardens they may be used to enliven dull spots in borders, as eye-catchers to close vistas, as pointers around the garden, to draw attention to a particular area or simply as decorative ornament. In every situation they may be employed to mark an entrance, such as either side of a doorway or positioned on gate piers, to furnish a terrace, patio or outside sitting or eating area, to line a pathway as a means of introducing a note of formality, or merely in a functional manner as a way of growing half hardy plants which will require winter protection.

Whatever, it must be remembered that pots and containers, once filled with soil and planted out, are permanently in need of care and attention. They must not be allowed to dry out. They will need feeding regularly throughout the season. Finally, attention to deadheading will encourage repeat flowers.

Displays of this kind can really only be effected with brightly coloured annuals which, if not fully hardy, may not be put outside until all danger of frost has passed.

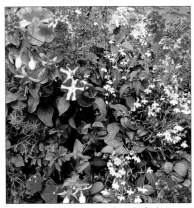

Hanging basket, crowded with fuchsia, petunia and lobelia, in a colour theme.

A gorgeous array of colour cleverly arranged in a single hanging basket.

Cheerful bedding plants join hands with the more sombre, permanent ivy around this window to form an integrated summer display. The containers have been disguised by the massed planting.

Such a composition can be re-arranged in
a moment as the mood takes you.

Setting these hot colours against a dark,
evergreen background shows them to
advantage.

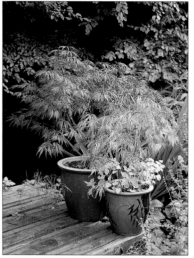

The glowing acers are well matched to
the dark pots which contain them.

Here the foliage of the agapanthus is as
important as the flower.

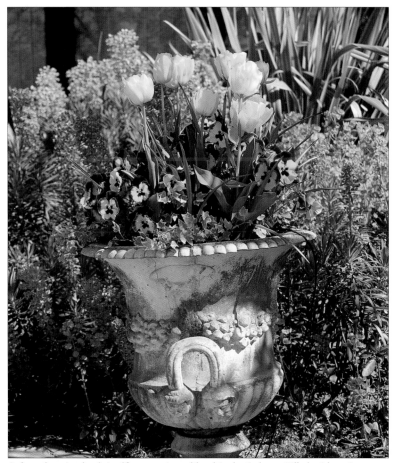

A formal setting lends itself to containers like this classical urn. Filled with spring tulips and complementary pansies, they never appear out of place.

This pot contains *Fritillaria imperialis* surrounded by blood-red tulips.

These two Versailles planters contain box pyramids as permanent structure.

Pots where the flower colour is severely restricted require the most confidence to create.

A sense of theatre in the placing of parrot tulips against this paintwork.

The formality of the trellis fence arranged in arches demands the kind of repeated planting which is shown here. The focal point of each planter is the box ball.

Huge box balls sit in these black painted planters to mark the approach.

Annual colour is added to these pots to surround perennial plantings. In time the shrubs will grow.

243

Relying in the main on two flowering plants with complementary foliage gives satisfying unity.

This collection of spring flowers is a delightful way in which to end a path.

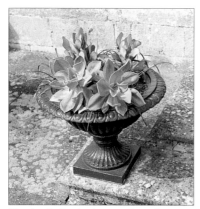

Planting is simple, the succulent chosen to pick up the colour of the paintwork.

Flower is restricted to the skimmias with box and ivy retaining colour all year.

Different plants with flowers from the same spectrum. Here the pinks tie in together.

An old copper pot, splendidly planted, is placed in the middle of a crossing point of two paths.

A charming mixture for the early spring gives the effect of a cottage garden in miniature.

A happy mixture in this collection which is sited on the treads of these steps.

Acknowledgements

Many of the photographs were taken in the author's garden, Arrow Cottage, Ledgemoor, Weobley. The publishers would also like to thank the many people and organizations whose gardens have appeared in this book, including the following:

Acton Beauchamp Roses, Worcester; Mr and Mrs A. Bambridge, Llanvair Kilgeddin, Abergavenny; Barnsley House, Barnsley, Cirencester; Burford House, Tenbury Wells; Chilcombe House, Chilcombe, Dorset; Dr A. and Dr L. Cox, Woodpeckers, Marlcliff, Bidford-on-Avon; Richard Edwards, Well Cottage, Blakemere; The Hon Mrs Peter Healing, The Priory, Kemerton; Hergest Croft, Kington; Kiftsgate Court, near Chipping Campden; Mr and Mrs D. Lewis, Ash Farm, Much Birch; Oxford Botanic Gardens; Mrs Richard Paice, Bourton House Garden, Bourton-on-the-Hill, Moreton-in-Marsh; Parham House, Parham; The Picton Garden, Colwall; Anthony Poulton, 21 Swinton Lane, Worcester; Powis Castle (National Trust); Royal Botanic Gardens, Kew; RHS Garden, Wisley; The Weir, Swainshill, Hereford (National Trust); Wakehurst Place (National Trust).

Index

Abutilon × *suntense* 92, 174
Acanthus spinosissimus 97
Acer campestre 192
Acer capillipes 214
Acer griseum 212
Acer japonicum 'Vitifolium' 193
Acer negundo 'Flamingo' 129
Acer obtusatum 194
Acer palmatum 195
Acer palmatum 'Heptalobum Osakazuki' 201
Acer palmatum 'Osakazuki' 46
Acer palmatum 'Senkaki' 195
Acer palmatum atropurpureum 194
Acer palmatum var. *dissectum* 'Garnet' 55
Achillea 35
Achillea grandifolia 155
Achillea millefolium 'Cerise Queen' 82
Achillea millefolium 'Lilac Beauty' 100
Aconites 230
Aconitum lycoctonum ssp. *vulparia* 167
Aconitum volubile 115
Adiantum venustum 122
Agapanthus 172, 240
Agapanthus Headbourne Hybrids 113
Ajuga reptans 'Pink Surprise' 220
Akebia quinata 53
Alcea 60
Alchemilla mollis 116
Allium aflatunense 'Purple Sensation' 94
Allium beesianum 113
Allium oreophilum 87
Allium sphaerocephalon 99
Alyssum 30, 220
Amaranthus caudatus 65
Amaryllis belladonna 87
Amelanchier 'Ballerina' 201
Anaphalis 153
Anaphalis margaritacea 144
Anchusa azurea 'Loddon Royalist' 110
Anemone appenina 174
Anemone blanda 'Pink Star' 87
Anemone blanda 'White Splendour' 136
Anemone fulgens 67

Anemone × *hybrida* 145
Anemone × *hybrida* 'Queen Charlotte' 87
Anemones 88
Angel's trumpets 235
Anisodontea capensis 235
Anthemis tinctoria 'E.C. Buxton' 171
Antirrhinum 'Black Prince' 67
Aquilegia bertolonii 218
Aquilegia vulgaris 'Adelaide Addison' 90
Aquilegia vulgaris 'Magpie' 159
Aralia elata 'Variegata' 128
Arbutus unedo 208
Arbutus unedo f. *rubra* 86
Argemone grandiflora 148
Artemisia 'Powis Castle' 152–153
Artemisia lactiflora Guizhou Group 146
Artemisia ludoviciana 'Valerie Finnis' 155
Arum italicum 'Pictum' 211
Asparagus 225
Asphodeline lutea 171
Aster frikartii 'Mönch' 99
Aster novi-belgii 'Goliath' 85
Asters 68, 187
Astilbe 'Amethyst' 87
Astilbe 'Deutschland' 148, 156
Astilbe 'Erica' 229
Astilbe 'Federsee' 67
Astrantia 139
Atriplex hortensis var. *rubra* 179
Aubrieta 220
Aucuba japonica 'Gold Dust' 129

Baby's breath 84
Balloon flower 113
Ballota 157
Bamboos 116
Bay 122
Beetroot 223
Bellflower 111
Berberis 90
Berberis thunbergii 207
Berberis thunbergii 'Atropurpurea' 201
Berberis thunbergii 'Bagatelle' 154

Berberis thunbergii 'Rose Glow' 67
Bergenia 116
Betula ermanii 214
Betula pendula 191
Betula utilis var. *jacquemontii* 215
Bidens 'Golden Goddess' 45
Birches 190
Bistort 223
Black Dragon 158
Black-eyed Susan 158, 236
Blue holly 115
Bluebells 71
Box 116
Brachyglottis (*Senecio*) 'Sunshine' 157
Brugmansia 235
Brunnera macrophylla 106
Brunnera macrophylla 'Dawson's White' 130
Buddleja alternifolia 103
Buddleja davidii 'Black Knight' 103
Buddleja davidii 'Dartmoor' 101
Bupleurum angulosum 120

Calendula 45
Callicarpa bodinieri var. *geraldii* 210
Callicarpas 88
Caltha palustris 32
Caltha palustris 'Flore Pleno' 228
Camassia 173
Camassia leichtlinii 109, 173
Camellia 'Cornish Snow' 148
Camellia 'Galaxie' 68
Camellia 'Water Lily' 69
Camellia japonica 'Nobilissima' 135
Camellia japonica 'Rubescens Major' 52
Camellias 68
Campanula arvatica 218
Campanula cochleariifolia 111
Campanula glomerata 'Superba' 103
Campanula lactiflora 169
Campanula latifolia 111, 172
Campanula latiloba 109
Campanula latiloba alba 142
Campanula persicifolia 142, 175
Candelabra primula 226
Cardoon 158
Carpenteria californica 148

Caryopteris × *clandonensis* 115
Catmints 90
Ceanothus 'Autumnal Blue' 112
Ceanothus 'Blue Mound' 108, 174
Ceanothus impressus 108
Ceanothus thyrsiflorus var. *repens* 92
Ceanothus × *thyrsiflorus* 174
Celandines 30
Centaurea macrocephala 36
Centranthus ruber 102
Centranthus ruber albus 139
Cephalaria gigantea 36
Ceratostigma plumbaginoides 114
Cercidiphyllum japonicum 193
Cercis canadensis 'Forest Pansy' 199
Chaenomeles 'Crimson and Gold' 67
Chaerophyllum hirsutum 'Roseum' 76
Chard 223
Cherries 68, 190
Chinese dogwood 207
Chinese lanterns 52
Chinese witch hazel 30
Chionodoxa 230
Chionodoxa luciliae 105, 215
Chives 222
Chocolate vine 53
Choisya 'Aztec Pearl' 173
Choisya ternata 'Sundance' 44
Christmas rose 135, 230
Cimicifuga simplex 147
Cineraria 155
Cistus 52
Cistus 'Paladin' 138
Cistus 'Silver Pink' 87
Cistus × *hybridus* 138
Clary 102
Clematis 68, 70
Clematis 'Blue Bird' 105
Clematis 'Comtesse de Bouchaud' 87
Clematis 'Gypsy Queen' 103
Clematis 'Haku-ôkan' 92
Clematis 'Jackmanii' 103
Clematis 'Lasurstern' 115
Clematis 'Nelly Moser' 70
Clematis 'Niobe' 57
Clematis 'Proteus' 91

Clematis alpina 'Willy' 70
Clematis cirrhosa 233
Clematis durandii 110
Clematis macropetala 70
Clematis macropetala 'Markham's Pink' 70
Clematis montana 174, 179
Clematis montana 'Grandiflora' 148
Clematis montana 'Tetrarose' 87
Clematis orientalis 'Bill Mackenzie' 45
Clematis texensis 'Gravetye Beauty' 67
Clematis texensis 'Princess of Wales' 81
Clematis viticella 'Etoile Violette' 98
Clematis viticella 'Little Nell' 143
Clematis viticella 'Madame Julia Correvon' 57, 178
Clematis viticella 'Margot Koster' 77
Clematis viticella 'Purpurea Plena Elegans' 102
Clematis viticella 'Venosa Violacea' 178
Cleome spinosa 86
Clivia miniata 236
Colchicum autumnale 'Album' 148
Colchicum speciosum 85
Columbines 159, 218
Cone flowers 145, 187
Consolida orientalis 115
Convolvulus sabatius 115
Coral Bark Maple 195
Coreopsis 187
Coreopsis verticillata 41, 171
Coreopsis verticillata 'Moonbeam' 41
Cornus alba 213
Cornus alba 'Elegantissima' 127
Cornus kousa 207
Cornus stolonifera 'Flaviramea' 213
Cortaderia selloana 149
Corydalis flexuosa 106
Cosmos 146
Cosmos 'Daydream' 87
Cosmos atrosanguineus 41
Cotinus 'Grace' 90
Cotinus coggygria 'Royal Purple' 51, 201
Cotoneaster frigidus 'Cornubia' 202
Cotoneaster frigidus 'Fructu Luteo' 202
Cotoneaster horizontalis 201
Cotoneaster salicifolius 'Exburyensis' 203
Cotoneasters 210

Cowslip 30, 31
Crab-apples 71
Cranesbill 70, 76, 137, 166
Crataegus × prunifolia 201
Crinum × powellii 83
Crinum × powellii 'Album' 146
Crocosmia 'Harlequin' 51
Crocosmia 'Lucifer' 61
Crocosmia masoniorum 51
Crocosmias 46
Crocus chrysanthus 'Cream Beauty' 45
Crocus chrysanthus 'Snow Bunting' 148
Crocus speciosus 103
Crocus tommasinianus 88
Crocuses 88
Crown imperials 46, 120
Cyclamen coum 231
Cyclamen hederifolium f. *album* 148
Cymbidium ruspex 'Ivory Queen' 237
Cynara cardunculus 152, 158
Cytisus 'Burkwoodii' 67

Daffodils 30
Dahlia 42, 147
Dahlia 'Bishop of Llandaff' 62
Daphne × burkwoodii 'Somerset' 72
Daphnes 68
Datura 235
Day lilies 46
Dead nettle 221
Delphinium 'Alice Artindale' 109
Delphinium belladonna 'Lamartine' 109
Deutzia × elegantissima 'Rosealind' 73
Dianthus 'Gravetye Gem' 67, 221
Dianthus 'Inshriach Dazzler' 218
Dianthus 'La Bourboule' 218
Dianthus 'Waithman Beauty' 221
Diascia cordata 221
Dicentra 'Bountiful' 67
Dierama pulcherrimum 87
Digitalis lutea 45
Digitalis parviflora 50
Digitalis × mertonensis 79
Disanthus cercidifolius 197
Dogwood 127, 190
Doronicum columnae 30

Echinacea purpurea 82, 187
Echinacea purpurea 'White Swan' 145
Echinops 171
Elaeagnus pungens 'Dicksonii' 44
Elaeagnus × ebbingei 'Limelight' 157
Elymus magellanicus 157
Enkianthus perulatus 196
Epimedium × youngianum 'Roseum' 71
Eranthis hyemalis 232
Eremurus stenophyllus ssp. *stenophyllus* 152
Erica carnea 230
Erigeron speciosus 'Pink Jewel' 96
Erinus alpinus 220
Eryngium 119
Eryngium × zabelii 156, 171
Eryngiums 116, 165, 175
Erythronium 'Citronella' 33
Erythronium californicum 'White Beauty' 136
Eschscholzia 175
Eschscholzia 'Cherry Ripe' 67
Eucalyptus gunnii 157
Eucalyptus pauciflora ssp. *niphophila* 212
Eucomis bicolor 121
Euonymus alatus 198
Euonymus cornutus var. *quinquecornutus* 209
Euonymus europaeus 209
Euonymus europaeus 'Red Cascade' 201, 209
Euonymus fortunei 'Emerald 'n' Gold' 44, 127
Euonymus fortunei 'Silver Queen' 127
Eupatorium purpureum 102
Euphorbia 94, 116
Euphorbia characias ssp. *wulfenii* 'Lambrook Gold' 117
Euphorbia denticulata 218
Euphorbia griffithii 'Fireglow' 54
Euphorbia polychroma 32, 118, 166
Euphorbia sikkimensis 121
Euphorbia × martinii 119
Euryops pectinatus 236
Evening primrose 43, 82, 223
Evergreen gum tree 212
Everlasting pea 77
Fairy's thimble 111
Felicia amelloides 110
Fennel 119

Ferns 116
Feverfew 164
Forget-me-nots 168
Forsythia 30
Fothergilla major 199
Fox-tail lily 152
Foxgloves 50, 79
Fremontodendron californicum 45
Fritillaria imperialis 242
Fritillaria imperialis 'Maxima Lutea' 45
Fritillaria meleagris 89
Fritillaria pyrenaica 219
Fuchsia 235
Fuchsia 'Checkerboard' 66
Fuchsia 'Dollar Princess' 60
Fuchsia 'Garden News' 82
Fuchsia 'Margaret' 103

Galanthus nivalis 231
Galtonias 116
Garrya elliptica 117
Gaura lindheimeri 155
Genista aetnensis 40
Gentiana acaulis 106
Gentiana lutea 169
Gentians 106
Geranium cinereum 'Ballerina' 76, 179
Geranium clarkei 'Kashmir Purple' 100
Geranium macrorrhizum 70
Geranium macrorrhizum 'Album' 137
Geranium magnificum 103
Geum 'Borisii' 46
Geum rivale 166
Geum rivale 'Leonard's Variety' 229
Gladiolus 147
Gladiolus communis byzantinus 186
Gladiolus papilio 101
Gladwin iris 211
Glory of the Snow 105, 215
Godetia 65
Golden hop 154
Golden rod 39
Golden sedge 226
Grape hyacinth 106, 181
Grasses 116
Great White Cherry 137

Gypsophila 47
Gypsophila 'Rosy Veil' 84

Hamamelis mollis 232
Hamamelis × *intermedia* 'Pallida' 30
Hardy plumbago 114
Heathers 230
Hebe cupressoides 'Boughton Dome' 123
Hebe × *divergens* 'Edinensis' 125
Hedera colchica 'Sulphur Heart' 130
Hedera helix 'Buttercup' 45
Hedera helix 'Goldheart' 130
Helenium 'Feuersiegel' 51
Helenium 'Golden Youth' 42
Helenium 'Moerheim Beauty' 63, 167
Helianthemum 'Supreme' 56
Helianthemums 166
Helianthus 171
Helianthus 'Lemon Queen' 43
Helianthus 'Monarch' 42
Helichrysum italicum 151
Heliotropium 'Marine' 103
Hellebores 72, 116, 159, 230
Helleborus argutifolius 117
Helleborus foetidus 'Wester Flisk' 230
Helleborus lividus 230, 233
Helleborus niger 135, 230
Helleborus orientalis 159, 230
Hemerocallis 'Catherine Woodbury' 87
Hemerocallis 'Stafford' 50
Hemerocallis lilio-asphodelus 45
Heuchera 'Greenfinch' 119
Heuchera micrantha 'Palace Purple' 153
Hibiscus syriacus 'Bluebird' 115
Hibiscus syriacus 'Diana' 148
Hibiscus syriacus 'Woodbridge' 65
Hibiscus trionum 45
Hippeastrum 87
Holly 44, 116, 128
Hollyhocks 60
Honesty 136
Honeysuckle 129
Hosta 'Frances Williams' 130
Houttuynia cordata 'Chameleon' 131
Humulus lupulus 'Aureus' 154
Hyacinthoides non-scriptus 170

Hydrangea aspera Villosa Group 100
Hydrangea macrophylla 80
Hydrangea macrophylla 'Ayesha' 81
Hydrangea macrophylla 'Blue Wave' 112
Hydrangeas 112
Hypericum × *inodorum* 'Elstead' 208

Ilex aquifolium 'Argentea Marginata Pendula'
  128
Ilex aquifolium 'Golden Queen' 44
Ilex meservae 115
Incarvillea delavayi 73
Inula magnifica 38
Ipomoea purpurea 115
Iris 'Black Swan' 158
Iris 'Mandarin' 94
Iris 'Pogo' 45
Iris chrysographes 103
Iris foetidissima 211
Iris missouriensis 107
Iris orientalis 140
Iris pseudacorus 119
Iris reticulata 103
Iris reticulata 'Harmony' 115, 231
Iris sibirica 'Helen Astor' 67
Iris sibirica 'Soft Blue' 107
Iris sibirica 'Summer Sky' 152
Iris unguicularis 231
Irises 35, 68
Irish yews 245
Ivies 116

Jacob's ladder 172
Japanese anemones 68
Japanese angelica tree 128
Japanese lily 83
Japanese maple 193
Jasmine 232
Jasminum nudiflorum 45, 232
Jasminum polyanthum 234
Jerusalem sage 164
Juniperus horizontalis 'Wiltonii' 115, 157

Kerria 170
Kerria japonica 'Pleniflora' 33
Killarney strawberry tree 208

Kirengeshoma palmata 45
Knapweed 36
Kniphofia 'Little Maid' 39
Kolkwitzia amabilis 'Pink Cloud' 87

Laburnum × *watereri* 'Vossii' 34
Lady's mantle 116
Lamium maculatum 'Wootton Pink' 221
Larix decidua 192
Larkspur 115
Lathyrus grandiflorus 77
Lathyrus latifolius 'White Pearl' 148
Lathyrus odoratus 'North Shore' 103
Laurus nobilis 122
Lavandula angustifolia 'Grappenhall' 103
Lavatera trimestris 'Mont Blanc' 148
Lavatera trimestris 'Pink Beauty' 87
Lavenders 68, 101
Leopard's bane 30
Lettuce 223
Leucanthemum × *superbum* 143
Leucothoe walteri 'Rainbow' 128
Lewisia cotyledon 218
Libertia formosa 138
Lilac 135
Lilies 68
Lilium 'Golden Splendor' 165
Lilium 'Journey's End' 67
Lilium 'Mont Blanc' 38
Lilium 'Olivia' 142
Lilium 'Pink Perfection' 87
Lilium regale 141
Lilium speciosum var. *rubrum* 83
Lilium tigrinum 'Pink' 87
Linum perenne 115
Linum rubrum 67
Liquidamber styraciflua 194
Liriope muscari 103
Lithodora diffusa 104
Lobelia 239
Lobelia 'Compliment Scarlet' 167
Lobelia 'Compliment' 64
Lobelia × *speciosa* 83
Lonicera japonica 'Aureoreticulata' 129
Lonicera × *brownii* 'Dropmore Scarlet' 56
Love-in-a-nist 115, 172

Love-lies-bleeding 65
Lunaria annua alba 136, 165
Lupins 35, 110
Lychnis chalcedonica 61
Lychnis coronaria 178
Lychnis coronaria 'Alba' 139
Lysichiton 226
Lysichiton americanus 30, 228
Lysichiton camtschatcensis 228
Lysimachia 39
Lysimachia ciliata 'Firecracker' 151
Lythrum salicaria 81

Magnolia grandiflora 147
Magnolia liliiflora 'Nigra' 67
Magnolia stellata 'Royal Star' 148
Magnolia × *soulangeana* 'Lennei' 69
Magnolias 68
Mahonia lomariifolia 45
Maidenhair fern 122
Mallows 68
Malus × *moerlandsii* 'Profusion' 71
Malus × *robusta* 'Red Sentinel' 205
Malus × *zumi* 'Golden Hornet' 203
Malva moschata alba 143, 175
Malva sylvestris mauritiana 93
Maples 190
Marguerites 183
Marigold 45, 46
Marsh marigold 30, 32, 228
Meconopsis cambrica 32, 168
Melianthus major 139
Mexican orange blossom 173
Michaelmas daisy 85, 99
Mimulus 168
Mimulus 'Orange Glow' 229
Miscanthus 'Silver Feather' 124
Montbretia 51
Morning glory 115
Mount Etna broom 40
Mountain ashes 203
Mulleins 152
Muscari armeniacum 181
Muscari aucheri 106
Muscari neglectum 115

Narcissus 'Flower Drift' 135
Narcissus 'Hawera' 31
Narcissus 'Thalia' 148
Narcissus bulbocodium 30, 233
Nasturtium 64, 223
Nepeta mussinii 90
Nepetas 171
Nerine bowdenii 84
Nerium oleander 237
Nicandra physalodes 114
Nicotiana 116, 121, 140
Nigella 172
Nigella damascena 115
Nyssa sylvatica 193

Obedient plant 87
Oenothera 'Fireworks' 40
Oenothera missouriensis 43
Oenothera speciosa 'Pink Petticoats' 82
Onions 225
Onopordum 150
Ophiopogon planiscapus 'Nigrescens' 158-159
Orach 179
Oriental poppies 47
Origanum laevigatum 103
Oxalis articulata 79
Oxalis articulata 'Foundation Pink' 79
Oxslips 30

Paeonia arietina 54
Paeonia delavayi var. *ludlowii* 34
Paeonia lactiflora 'Docteur H. Barnsby' 57
Paeonia lactiflora 'Monsieur Jules Elie' 73
Paeonia mlokosewitschii 32
Paeonia suffruticosa 'Sitifukujin' 72
Pampas grass 149, 194
Papaver commutatum 'Lady Bird' 67
Papaver orientale 47
Papaver orientale 'Beauty of Livermere' 56
Papaver rhoeas 77
Paperbark maple 212
Parthenocissus henryana 201
Parthenocissus quinquefolia 200
Pasque flowers 88
Passiflora caerulea 100
Passion flowers 100

Pelargonium 235
Pelargonium 'Lord Bute' 60
Pelargonium 'Madame Layal' 235
Penstemon 'Blackbird' 94
Penstemon 'Catherine de la Mare' 94
Penstemon 'Papal Purple' 94
Penstemon 'Red Knight' 61
Penstemon glaber 94
Penstemon pulchellus 218
Penstemon venustus 76
Peonies 54
Periwinkle 85
Pernettya (*Gaultheria*) *mucronata* 210
Perovskia atriplicifolia 114
Petunia 239
Petunia 'Plum Purple' 103
Phacelia campanularia 115
Phlomis fruticosa 164
Phlox 'Chattahoochee' 96
Phlox 'Mother of Pearl' 87
Phlox paniculata 'Fairy's Petticoat' 79
Phlox paniculata 'White Admiral' 148
Phloxes 79
Phormium tenax 124
Photinia davidiana 208
Phygelius 169
Physalis 52
Physostegia virginiana 87
Picea pungens 'Koster' 115
Pinks 68, 221
Pittosporum × *tenuifolium* 158
Plantain lily 130
Platycodon grandiflorus mariesii 113
Plumbago capensis 237
Polygonum bistorta 223
Polystichum setiferum 'Divisilobum' 122
Poppies 32
Portuguese laurel 116
Potentilla 175
Potentilla atrosanguinea 67
Potentilla fruticosa 40
Prairie cord grass 131
Primroses 30
Primula auricula 31
Primula florindae 45, 228
Primula japonica 'Miller's Crimson' 67

Primula pulverulenta 227
Primula sieboldii 227
Primula veris 31
Primula vialii 74
Primulas 46, 72
Prunella grandiflora 'Pink Loveliness' 76
Prunus 'Tai Haku' 137
Prunus cerasifera 'Nigra' 69
Prunus lusitanica 116
Prunus serrula 214
Prunus tenella 'Firehill' 72
Prunus × *yedoensis* 'Yoshino' 195
Pseudolarix amabilis 190
Pseudosasa japonica 124
Pulmonaria 72
Pulmonaria angustifolia 'Munstead Blue' 115
Pulmonaria officinalis 'Sissinghurst White'
    148
Pulsatilla vulgaris 89, 219
Pulsatilla vulgaris rubra 219
Pyracanthas 207
Pyrus salicifolia 'Pendula' 134, 157

Red hot pokers 116
Rheum alexandrae 119
Rhodiola rosea 35
Rhododendron augustinii 89
Rhododendron kaempferi 53
Rhododendron luteum 45
Rhododendron yakushimanum 87
Rhus glabra 'Laciniata' 201
Rhus typhina 198
Rock roses 166
Romneya coulteri 148
Rosa 'Albertine' 78
Rosa 'Alchymist' 49
Rosa 'Allen Chandler' 67
Rosa 'Anne Harkness' 48
Rosa 'Baron Girod de l'Ain' 59
Rosa 'Bleu Magenta' 95
Rosa 'Blue Boy' 95
Rosa 'Brown Velvet' 49
Rosa 'Canary Bird' 162
Rosa 'Climbing Iceberg' 148
Rosa 'Crimson Shower' 59
Rosa 'Dearest' 87

Rosa 'Frühlingsgold' 34
Rosa 'Graham Thomas' 37
Rosa 'Hunter' 59
Rosa 'Iceberg' 140
Rosa 'Iris Webb' 48
Rosa 'Just Joey' 48
Rosa 'Madame Caroline Testout' 87
Rosa 'May Queen' 74
Rosa 'Mermaid' 45
Rosa 'Pink Elizabeth Arden' 75
Rosa 'Princess Marie' 78
Rosa 'Raubritter' 78
Rosa 'Scarlet Fire' 67
Rosa 'Schoolgirl' 48
Rosa 'Sweet Dream' 49
Rosa 'Veilchenblau' 96
Rosa 'Zigeunerknabe' 95
Rosa moyesii 'Geranium' 55, 206
Rosa rugosa 'Alba' 148, 164, 199
Rosa xanthina 'Canary Bird' 33
Rosemary 108, 222
Roses 68
Rosmarinus officinalis 108
Rosmarinus repens 'Severn Sea' 115
Round-headed leek 99
Rowans 190
Rudbeckia 158
Rudbeckia fulgida 'Goldsturm' 43, 187
Runner beans 225
Russian sage 114
Ruta graveolens 151

Sage 97, 125, 222
Salix alba vitellina 'Britzensis' 46, 213
Salvia horminum 102
Salvia officinalis 125
Salvia patens 111
Salvia sclarea var. *turkestanica* 97
Salvia splendens 64
Salvia uliginosa 115
Salvia viridis 183
Salvias 171
Sambucus nigra 'Guincho Purple' 51
Santolina chamaecyparissus 'Lemon Queen' 39, 167
Santolina elegans 218
Saponaria vicaria 'Alba' 87

Scabiosa 'Chile Black' 158
Scabious 169
Schizostylis coccinea 67
Schizostylis coccinea 'Sunrise' 84
Scilla mischtschenkoana 105
Scilla non-scripta 71
Scilla sibirica 'Spring Beauty' 115
Sedges 116
Sedum 153
Sedum 'Autumn Joy' 67
Sedum rhodiola 35
Sempervivums 220
Shasta daisies 143
Shield fern 122
Shoo-fly plant 114
Siberian bugloss 106
Sidalcea candida 139
Silver birch 191
Sisyrinchium striatum 'Aunt May' 175
Skimmia japonica 211
Skimmia japonica 'Veitchii' 211
Skimmias 244
Skunk cabbages 228
Smoke bush 90
Smyrnium perfoliatum 119
Snake bark maples 214
Snake's head fritillary 89
Snowdrops 230
Solanum crispum 'Glasnevin' 103
Sorbus 'Joseph Rock' 203
Sorbus 'Winter Cheer' 204
Sorbus alnifolia 193
Sorbus cashmiriana 'Rosiness' 204
Sorbus sargentiana 196, 204
Sorbus vilmorinii 204
Spartina pectinata 'Aureomarginata' 131
Spearmint 223
Spider flower 86
Spindle berries 190
Spurge 117
Squills 105
Stachys byzantina 67, 151
Stachys byzantina 'Silver Carpet' 154
Staghorn sumach 198
Stipa barbata 'Silver Feather' 152
Stipa tenuissima 121

Stocks 68
Strawberry tree 86
Stuartia sinensis 214
Sumachs 190
Syringa 'Elinor' 103
Syringa vulgaris 135

Tanacetum 153
Tanacetum (*Chrysanthemum*) *parthenium* 'Aureum' 36
Tanacetum haradjanii 156
Tanacetum parthenium 164
Tanacetum vulgare 125
Tansy 156
Thermopsis montana 35
Thunbergia alata 236
Thymes 93
Thymus 'Doone Valley' 131
Tiarella cordifolia 137
Tithonia 'Yellow Torch' 45
Tobacco plants 116, 140
Tradescantia × *andersoniana* 'Pauline' 87
Tree peonies 34, 72
Trifolium rubens 93
Tropaeolum majus 64
Tropaeolum speciosum 58
Tropaeolum tuberosum 'Ken Aslett' 50
Tulipa 'Black Parrot' 158
Tulipa 'Blue Heron' 90
Tulipa 'China Pink' 74
Tulipa 'First Lady' 103
Tulipa 'Golden Melody' 180
Tulipa 'Purissima' 136
Tulipa 'Queen of Sheba' 67
Tulipa 'Queen of the Night' 158
Tulipa 'Spring Green' 118
Tulipa 'West Point' 45
Tulipa 'White Triumphator' 148
Tulipa greigii 'Red Riding Hood' 53
Tulipa sprengeri 46, 55
Tulips 54
Tupelo 193

Valerian 102, 139
Valeriana phu 'Aurea' 170
Veratrum nigrum 122

Verbascum nigrum 167, 169
Verbascum olympicum 152
Verbena 'Aveyron' 86
Verbena bonariensis 88, 99, 183, 187
Veronica peduncularis 'Georgia Blue' 115
Veronica pinnata 'Blue Eyes' 107
Veronica teucrium 'Shirley Blue' 107
Veronicastrum virginicum 144
Viburnum betulifolium 206
Viburnum × *bodnantense* 'Dawn' 87
Viburnum opulus 206
Viburnum opulus 'Xanthocarpum' 203
Viburnum plicatum 'Mariesii' 137, 197
Viburnum recognitum 198
Viburnums 68
Vinca 85
Viola 225
Viola 'Bowles' Black' 159
Viola 'Roscastle Black' 158
Viola 'Ruby Queen' 67
Viola cornuta 175
Viola odorata 'Princess of Wales' 103
Violets 88, 159

Virginia creeper 200
Vitis coignetiae 201
Vitis vinifera 'Brandt' 201

Wallflowers 46, 181
Water avens 229
Water lilies 227
Weigela florida 'Foliis Purpureis' 87
Weigela florida 'Variegata' 126
Welsh poppy 32, 168
Whitebeams 190
Winter jasmine 45
Wisteria floribunda 92, 179
Wisteria floribunda 'Alba' 138
Wisteria floribunda 'Violacea Plena' 103
Witch hazels 232

Yellow flag irises 226
Yoshino Cherry 195

Zantedeschia aethiopica 'Crowborough' 156
Zauschneria californica 62
Zinnia 62